Digging Deeper: *Getting far more out of God's Word than you ever have before.*

By Bill F. Korver

www.metakoi.com

Copyright 2021 3rd edition Bill F. Korver. All rights reserved. No portion of this book may be Reproduced, stored in a retrieval system, or transmitted in any form or by any other means electronic, mechanical, photocopy, recording or other except for brief quotations in printed reviews, without the written consent of the publisher.

Published by Metakoi Publishing and Lightning Source (a subsidiary of Ingram Content Group), 1246 Heil Quaker Boulevard, La Vergne, TN USA 37086

All Scripture quotations, unless otherwise indicated, are taken from the Holy Bible, New American Standard (NASB 1995) version, copyright by the Lockman Foundation.

Korver, Bill F.
Digging Deeper: Getting More Out of God's Word Than You Ever Have Before.
3rd edition

ISBN:978-0-9905783-0-7

1. Bible Study 2. Korver, Bill 3. Hermeneutics

Printed in the United States of America

Dedication

This book is dedicated to two men, Dr. James B. Raiford and Rick Oglesby. Dr. Raiford taught me the basic principles found in the following pages while I was a student of his while I was in Bible College. Further, he modeled them as I labored alongside him as my pastor and mentor in local church ministry for six years. Rick Oglesby was a fellow student with me long ago. He demonstrated unusual skills and soon outdistanced the rest of us in class and ministry effectiveness. Years later he put some thoughts down on paper and graciously let me use them as a foundation to build upon. The foundation both these men laid resulted in the book you hold in your hands. Both men have consistently practiced the principles taught herein. I am blessed to have been able to be mentored and befriended by them both. They are choice servants of the King, Jesus!

Additionally, this volume is dedicated to the hundreds of students, past, present, and future, that I have been privileged, or by God's grace, will be privileged to teach while serving at Carolina College of Biblical Studies. It is my prayer each will keep *Digging Deeper*.

Introduction

Welcome to *How to Study the Bible*! This course will be a challenging, eye-opening and life-changing experience as you apply yourself faithfully to studying the Bible. The *How to Study the Bible* course is the signature course of Carolina College of Biblical Studies. We believe it is the most important one we offer because if we teach a student how to interpret the Word of God, then he/she will have their life transformed in preparation to be used by God for effective and fruitful ministry. When I look back at my own thirteen years of biblical higher education, I can say, without hesitation, that the most important classes I ever took were those that taught me the skills of Bible interpretation.

The following notes are specifically designed with you in mind. You will find the paragraphs in your notes numbered to make it easier for you to ask questions and to study.

You were provided a Bible for this course. This allows everyone to read and study the same translation: New American Standard (NASB). This Bible will also prevent you from peeking at marginal and study notes. You will be forced to depend solely on your constantly growing skills and so improve your efforts.

Finally, review sheets are provided for you and can be found at the end of each chapter. God bless you as you enter the life-long adventure of serious Bible Study.

Bill F. Korver, D. Min.

President, Carolina College of Biblical Studies

WHY THIS STUDY?

Although the following is not a complete list, many good reasons exist for studying the Bible. Let's start with a few reasons for learning how to study the Bible on your own:

1. Position does not equal <u>*understanding.*</u>

In John 3:1-17, John records a conversation between Jesus and a man named Nicodemus. The reader is informed that Nicodemus was a Pharisee, a religious leader, and a ruler of the Jewish people. During the conversation Jesus told him that no person would see the kingdom unless he was first born again or born from above (given life by God). It is clear from reading the interaction between Jesus and Nicodemus that he did not understand what Jesus had said. After a bit of back and forth in the conversation, Jesus finally said, "*Are you **the teacher** of Israel and do not understand these things?*" (John 3:10, emphasis mine). In the first century, it was possible to be a spiritual leader and teacher and not understand or know something as basic as how to be saved. If it happened in Jesus' day, you can be sure it happens in our day. Just because a person is a church leader does not mean he/she understands basic Bible truth. Several years ago, I had a student in a Bible college setting who informed me he had been a pastor for seven years. Yet it became clear as the class progressed, he did not have even a rudimentary understanding of the Bible. Being a pastor or teacher does not mean one knows what God has said only a careful and consistent study of the Word of God will do that.

By my count, on eleven occasions the New Testament Gospels record that Jesus said to the religious leaders of His day, "*Have you not read…?*" Whether or not they had actually read God's Word, the implication was that they did not understand what God had said. To be sure they read and reflected upon what the scholars taught and wrote, they knew well what the leading teachers from the past had said. The problem was they did not know what God said!

This problem was not merely a New Testament problem. It was common in the Old Testament too. Notice the prophet Jeremiah's words to the leaders of his day: *"Thus says the LORD of hosts, 'Do not listen to the words of the prophets who are prophesying to you. They are leading you into futility; they speak a vision of their own imagination, not from the mouth of the LORD'"* (Jeremiah 23:16).

2. Those who teach others the scriptures will be held to a higher standard.
James 3:1 states, *"Let not many of you become teachers, my brethren, knowing that as such, we will incur a stricter judgment."* The human writer of the book we call James was the half-brother of Jesus. He warned his readers that rather than clamor to teach they should be very careful before agreeing to a teaching responsibility or position. The reason for his warning? People believe what teachers say. Whether what the teacher says is accurate of not, people believe that when a person in the position of a teacher speaks, they will be hearing from God. Think of how counter-cultural this is. In our day, in the evangelical church, we "undersell" the position of teacher with how we recruit potential teachers. Imagine the Sunday School Superintendent (Bob) approaching a recruit (Mary). Here's how the conversation often goes:

Bob: "Mary would you consider teaching the junior high girls' Sunday School class?"

Mary: "I'm not sure Bob, I don't think I am qualified. I've never taught."

Bob: "Oh that's okay. You can do it. It's easy."

Mary: "I have never taught and don't know the Bible very well. I was only recently saved myself."

Bob: "There's nothing to it. We'll provide you with a teacher's manual. All you need to do is just show up and read it. There's no preparation involved."

I think James would have strolled into a prospective teacher's meeting with the following words, "Ladies and gentlemen, thanks for coming today. Our church is very much in need of some very fine teachers; however, many of you may not be up to the task and may not be qualified. It is a very important ministry that will take a good deal of preparation. Like the Marines, we and the Lord are looking for a few good men and women."

You cannot be a good teacher of the Word of God without knowing what God has said, and you cannot know what God has said if you have not studied His Word. Lesson preparation begins with a careful study of the Word of God, not a quick perusal of a teacher's manual. Those who wish to teach the Word of God need to know and practice the principles taught in this book.

3. God's command to be _diligent_ and _accurate_ with His Word.
The command of 2 Timothy 2:15: "*Be diligent to present yourself approved to God as a workman who does not need to be ashamed, handling accurately the word of truth*." In part, Paul tells Timothy to be careful to handle the Bible accurately. In another place, the imagery used is that the Bible is a sword that is living and active and can *"cut to the marrow and bone of the thoughts and intents of the heart"* (Hebrews 4:12). Our culture does not use swords, so let me illustrate what Paul is saying by using a scalpel. A trained surgeon can handle one with great skill to help bring healing, to prevent the spread of a serious illness and more. An untrained person or one with evil intensions can use the same scalpel to kill or maim others. Likewise, the sword of God can be misused to the destruction of self and others. These notes are designed, in part, to instruct you on how to be skillful in the use of your sword.

4. The rise of _relativism_.
The rise of the "there is no right answer" or "everybody's right" mentality.
It's not unusual to be in a small group or Sunday school setting where multiple interpretations of a given verse or text of Scripture are given while many nod their

heads in approval as if all answers are equally good ones. Imagine how absurd it would be to do the same thing in a math class. For example, 7 + 6 = 13. All other answers are incorrect. Some may be closer to correct than others (e.g., 14 is better than 27, but both are still incorrect). The same concept applies to geography (there are mountain ranges in specific places), history (President George Washington served at a specific period of time), the legal system (lying is perjury), etc. I do not intend to communicate that I have all the right answers/interpretations, merely that there is only one correct interpretation to any given passage of Scripture. These notes are designed to assist you in determining the correct interpretation to any passage of Scripture.

5. The Joy of *discovery*.

Years ago- 1975 to be exact - Oletta Wald wrote a little book entitled *The Joy of Discovery*. It was a text I used as a freshman in Bible College. There is something great about digging into the riches of God's Word and discovering truth that you are convinced has never been discovered by anyone in history!

When I was a little boy in the 1960's in a large family with few financial means, I remember my five siblings and me playing at a park behind our house in Arlington, Texas. My oldest sister went into the women's restroom and came out seconds later excited. She had found a twenty-dollar bill! I was glad for her and a little excited, thinking she might pass on some of her newfound riches to me. She, on the other hand, was ecstatic. Why? It was her discovery and therefore her money. Something wonderful happens when you discover truth on your own.

6. *Intimacy* with God.

In relationships, intimacy is developed through conversation. When I pastored, I knew a couple who had both been widowed and met over the phone through mutual friends. They courted for months, running up huge long-distance phone bills (before cell phone days with unlimited minutes). The man proposed to the woman, having never met her face to face. The same sort of thing happens when you spend time with God in His Word. You get to know His heart. You see His faithfulness, grace, and more (Ps. 119).

One last thought before we dive in. Learning to study the Bible is, in some ways, like learning to ride a bicycle. You will never learn either skill by reading about the subject. You learn how to ride a bicycle and how to study the Bible by doing it. With that in mind, each chapter will have homework assignments to go along with what is being taught and learned each week. When I was a boy, growing up in a blue-collar home where resources were few, no kid on our street had training wheels to help them learn how to ride a bicycle. You just "crashed and burned" until you got the hang of riding. Coupled with that the fact that most kids then didn't own a bike, so we shared with several siblings. When I was about six years old, a girl from up the street came to play with two of my sisters. She parked her bike in the front yard and went to the back yard to play. I yelled out, "Can I borrow your bicycle?" To which one of my loving sisters responded, "You don't even know how to ride a bike." Undeterred I climbed on and attempted to ride. After a few tries, I actually got the hang of it and started down the street! About three houses past my parents there was a sharp turn in the road, and it dawned on me that I had no idea of how to turn a bicycle while still maintaining my balance. Problem solved. I just stopped the bike, hopped off, picked it up, turned it around, jumped back on, and headed in the direction I had just come from. By the time I was ten years old, four years later, I could "pop a wheelie" (ride on the back tire, with the front tire suspended in the air) all the way around a half-mile oval. What changed in four years? I can assure you it was not reading books on how to ride a bicycle. It was due to the fact I spent so much time riding one.

The same will happen to your ever-improving Bible study skills. As you practice, you will improve. Happy riding! If you faithfully and consistently practice the principles taught here, you will rapidly progress from where you are as a Bible student to an advanced learner.

A note of caution might be in order: the goal of Bible study is not ***merely*** to know the Bible better, but to have your life transformed by God as you interact with and obey His living Word. Certainly, God does not value ignorance of His Word, but it is not the goal of Bible study to know more facts than you used to and more than others. The goal of Bible study should be ***life-transformation***. As we study, God, through His indwelling Holy Spirit, shows us changes that we need to make in relation to our thinking about Him, our value system, our interaction with others, and more. Ready to set out on a journey of life-transformation? Fasten your seatbelt!

The Principles For Reading the Bible Well

Mapping Out a Clear Course to Understanding the Bible

Table of Contents

1. Do you Read Well? — Page 17
2. The Principle of Plain Meaning — Page 33
3. The Principle of Context pt. 1 — Page 43
4. The Principle of Context pt. 2 — Page 53
5. The Principle of Context pt. 3 — Page 61
6. Principles of Grammar pt.1 — Page 69
7. Principles of Grammar pt.2 — Page 81
8. The Principle of Word Meaning pt. 1 — Page 89
9. The Principle of Word Meaning pt. 2 — Page 101
10. Literally? Understanding Figurative Language — Page 109
11. The Principle of Related Scripture — Page 117
12. Observing the Text — Page 127
13. Interpreting the Text — Page 133
14. Applying the Text — Page 141
15. The Rearview Mirror: Summarizing Digging Deeper — Page 147

Appendices — Page 155

Chapter 1
DO YOU READ WELL?

A character in Alice in Wonderland said, "A word means precisely what I want it to mean–nothing more and nothing less." For you to treat words this way would be foolish and chaotic. To treat biblical words in this way would be tragic. In studying the Scriptures, you must know how to determine what God says, not what it means to you. The guiding principles to understanding the Scripture are the subject of this course.

The interpretation of Scripture is a fascinating and rewarding experience. Proper interpretation of the Bible is the ***privilege*** and ***responsibility*** of every Christian. God's Word calls upon every believer not only to read and understand its message, but also to apply its truth. One does not have to be a pastor or theologian to learn how to interpret the Bible well. After all, the Bible was written to meet the spiritual needs of the ordinary person.

I use the word ***privilege*** because there are more than one billion people on planet earth today who are not able to purchase a Bible to read in their "heart language," even if they had enough money to do so. The reason? It simply is not available. In the West, we are blessed to have many good translations, and they can be purchased very inexpensively. A person with no money can also get one free of charge from a fine ministry such as *Gideons International*.

Long ago there lived a man named John Wycliffe (1328-1384). He believed that common people should have the Bible in their own language. Since he was English, he decided to translate the Bible into the English language. His actions eventually cost him his life due to the hatred of the state church which didn't want the average person reading God's Word. Many others have paid the ultimate price to make God's Word available to us in English.

Additionally, it is a believer's **responsibility** to study the Word. It is not a task to be reserved for a pastor alone. During the middle ages, in Europe, the Bible was only available in Latin, and only the clergy read Latin. Consequently, God's people became vulnerable to false teachings. God wants His people to know what He has said, so He revealed Himself to us and holds us responsible for being obedient to its truth. It will never be acceptable to God, when each believer stands before Him to give an account of his life to say, "That's what my pastor/teacher/professor/friend said." God will want to know how you responded to His Word.

I. WHAT IT TAKES TO READ THE BIBLE WELL

A. The foundational prerequisite for being a Bible student is to be **regenerated** or born again by the Holy Spirit. Without new birth, one cannot understand God's Word. Only a spiritually living person is able to comprehend spiritual truth.

Jesus answered and said to him, "Truly, truly, I say to you, unless one is born again, he cannot see the kingdom of God" (John 3:3).
"But a natural man does not accept the things of the Spirit of God; for they are foolishness to him, and he cannot understand them, because they are spiritually appraised. But he who is spiritual appraises all things, yet he himself is appraised by no man" (1 Cor. 2:14-15).

Have you ever noticed that the unsaved people in your life don't understand a lot of what believers do and value? For example, an unsaved person thinks going to church on Sunday morning is a perfectly good "waste" of a morning when they can sleep in, go hunting, fishing, or watch a ball game. Additionally, they think it is foolish to give away hard earned money to a church or mission organization. These are merely a few instances of the natural man's thinking as it relates to matters that are important to the follower of Christ. Most importantly, the unsaved person does not comprehend the need for a Savior.

This is a great time to be sure that you are spiritually alive. The Bible states that if you believe on the Lord Jesus Christ, you will be saved. His sinless life provides the perfect righteousness that God requires of you. Jesus' death satisfies God's wrath against your sin because He died as your substitute. Finally, God was so pleased with who Jesus is and what He did that He raised Jesus from the dead. His resurrection proves He is Savior King and that God was satisfied with His work. You must trust Jesus to receive His righteousness in exchange for your sin and His life in return for your death. In order to be saved you don't need to be baptized, pray a certain prayer, or turn over a new leaf. You do need to believe Jesus Christ's promise for eternal life (John 6:47; Acts 16:31).

Have you trusted Jesus Christ? If you haven't, you can do so right now right where you are. If you do, tell Him that you believe He is your Savior and thank Him for your forgiveness. Tell your teacher that you have done so-she will want to celebrate with you. If you have trusted Jesus sometime before now, stop right now and thank Him for being the object of your faith, and thank God for His grace to you!

B. In addition to new birth, good Bible students have three vital attitudes. Read the following Scriptures carefully.

1. The Bible student must have a ***desire*** for God's truth.

"Blessed are those who hunger and thirst for righteousness, for they shall be satisfied" Matt. 5:6.

"As the deer pants for the water brooks, so My soul pants for You, O God." Ps. 42:1

When I was in high school, I essentially hated science. In order to graduate from high school, I had to take a biology course. Years have passed since that course, and I do not remember one thing I learned in that class. This sad fact was not the fault of the teacher, it was due to the fact that I had no desire to learn. Perhaps you have a similar story? Did you have a class in high school that you HAD to take but didn't want to? The **desire** to know God's Word is crucial to gaining understanding.

2. The Bible student must be **_dependent_** upon the Holy Spirit.

"For to us God revealed them through the Spirit; for the Spirit searches for all things, even the depths of God... which things we speak, not in words taught by human wisdom, but in those taught by the Spirit, combining spiritual thought with spiritual words" (1 Cor. 2:10, 13).

"But when He, the Spirit of truth, comes, He will guide you unto all the truth; for He will not speak on His own initiative, but whatever He hears, He will speak; and He will disclose to you what is to come" (John 16:13).

In Psalm 119:18, the human author models this dependence when he writes, *"Open my eyes, that I may behold wonderful things from Thy law."*

When I was a pastor, I would start preparing my upcoming sermons on Monday morning. I had a self-imposed deadline of Thursday at noon. By that time, I had to get the sermon outline to my secretary for her to type the bulletin. At times I wrongly believed that, due to the excellent biblical training I received, I could study the biblical text and prepare a sermon on my own. While I never said it, my life was lived as though to say, "Holy Spirit, you can take a break. I can do this on my own, after all I have a good mind and received a great training, even had three courses in Hermeneutics." Sadly, it often took until Tuesday or Wednesday of the week when I had become desperate that I would ask God's Spirit to open my eyes to the truth. When I demonstrated this dependence, it was uncanny how the Spirit would illumine the text - often within a matter of minutes. What had been lacking on Monday and Tuesday? A complete lack of dependence on the Spirit. I had an arrogant attitude. I believed that I could interpret the text due to my training in Bible college, seminary, and graduate school. The Bible clearly states, *"Pride goes before destruction and a haughty spirit before stumbling"* (Prov. 16:18).

3. The Bible student must have **_diligence_** in the study of God's Word.
"Give diligence to present thyself approved unto God, a workman that needs not to be ashamed, handling aright the word of truth" (2 Tim. 2:15).

Note how wise king Solomon instructed his son regarding the search for wisdom from God: *"If you seek her (wisdom) as silver, and search for her as for hidden treasures"* (Prov. 2:4), and *"For its profit is better than the profit of silver, and its gain than fine gold. She is more precious than jewels and nothing you desire compares with her"* (Prov. 3:14, 15).

More than twenty years ago, a story ran in a popular magazine about a man who had discovered more than 1 billion dollars' worth of gold from a sunken pirate ship in water only about 100 feet deep! Who wouldn't like to find that much money in shallow water? Upon closer glance, however, the story went on to say that the man had searched diligently for more than two decades. He had invested millions of dollars in the search and had lost two family members at sea in stormy weather.

This attitude is the determination, the grit, to do the hard work and invest the necessary time to do Bible study. In the verses listed above from Proverbs, Solomon likened wisdom to gold, silver, and precious gems. I often ask my students if they have ever just stumbled over a big gold brick in their yard. They always answer, "no." Then I ask, "If you wanted to get gold and you couldn't afford to buy it and you refused to steal it, how would you come into possession of it?" They always answer, "You would have to dig for it, mine for it." It would take hard work, moving yards of dirt to find some small nuggets of what is considered a precious metal. So, too, the student of the Word must expend some effort to discover the rich treasure that the Bible has to offer.

When I was a boy, every summer our family would travel from Oklahoma, where we lived, to Iowa, where our roots and extended family were. My Uncle Calvin was a farmer. He farmed crops, as well as kept dairy cows. Before he purchased machines, he milked by hand every day. We would go by his farm, and he'd be seated on a short three-legged stool, milking away. He'd usually grab an udder and spray me with milk too. I often relate this story to my students and ask them, "Which is the most important leg on a three-legged stool?" Of course, the correct answer is they all are! Ever try to sit on a two-legged stool? It is also the same with Bible study: all three vital attitudes are important. One dare not neglect any one of them.

B. The Bible Reader Needs Two Primary Skills

Many brothers and sisters in Christ possess the previous attitudes yet disagree on what the Bible teaches. Why? Because we lack two basic skills.

1. First, we must ***read well***. Since the Bible is a book, we must read well to understand it properly. The basic skill of reading is one that you can never learn too well. Read, read, read! Repeatedly read before you start to interpret! Read not merely to see words on a page, but to understand what you are reading. Only when one understands what she has read has she read well. It is not a matter of merely seeing words on a page, but also comprehending what the words mean.

Much of this course will develop the concept of reading well. Two helpful resources are *How to Read a Book* by Mortimer Adler and *Living By The Book*, by Hendricks and Hendricks.

2. Most disputes over the Bible are related to the question of meaning. Reading the Bible is one thing, but ***understanding*** its meaning is quite another. "Do I understand you?" is our primary concern as we look into the Bible. In the following pages, we will outline some principles and practices that will enable you to say, "I read you and understand you clearly!"

II. Some Benefits to Reading the Bible Well

Suppose you were to apply for a job and were granted an interview with your prospective boss. In the course of the interview, issues are raised, such as job description and hours of work. It would not be out of line to ask about the salary and benefits, would it? Of course not! If the supervisor said that you would be expected to work but receive no benefits or that the benefits were not motivating ($1.50 per hour), you would never work at that business. If there are no benefits to Bible study, who would do the work? Fortunately, there are many benefits. The following is a short list of *some* of them.

    A.   You will only **_grow steadily_** when you read the Bible well. First Peter 2:2, states, "*Like newborn babes, long for the pure milk of the word, that by it you may **_grow_** in respect to salvation.*" The Bible is God's primary means of causing your growth. Indeed, you cannot and will not develop spiritually without regular intake of the Bible. The apostle Peter, the writer of this verse, likens believers to newborn babies. Newborns need food, and not just any food, they need milk. When they have a regular intake of it they grow quickly. It's not unusual for a baby to double its weight in a matter of a few months and grow several inches longer too.

           To state it in the negative, when a baby turns his head away from a bottle of milk, even though too young to talk, a good parent instinctively knows something is wrong - the baby has lost its appetite. Far too many Christians have little or no appetite for the Word. When one has a regular intake of the Word, through reading, meditation, and memorization, amazing growth happens!

           When I was in college, I studied alongside a student who had recently come to faith, while I had been a believer for twelve years. He spent many hours each afternoon and late into the night reading and studying his Bible, and it wasn't too long before he had surpassed the rest of us concerning spiritual growth. He had a steady diet of milk. We did not.

    B.   You will only develop **_maturity_** through regular biblical application (Hebrews 5:11-14). Immature children are very naïve. They are gullible and subject to believe nearly anything. When I was a boy growing up in a blue-collar home with very little extras, I would occasionally have a nickel to spend. A few blocks away from my house was a dime store that had a candy counter where candy could be purchased for a penny per piece. On the route to the store with the nickel, there was a family with a boy who was younger than I was. His parents both worked and forbade him from leaving his yard in the summer while they were gone to work. By our neighborhood standards, his family was rich. We drank water out of the garden hose; they always had ice cold *Pepsi* in the sixteen-ounce bottles. We never had chips; they always had *Fritos* on hand (my favorite). On occasion I would pass Nelson's house on my way to the store. If he was in the front yard, I'd call him over to the street and ask if he had any money. When he emptied his pockets, I would offer to trade my big coin (nickel) for his little coin (dime), which he would agree to do. On the way back from the store I would always make sure to have at least two pieces of red licorice in my bag of candy (my favorite and Nelson's too). He would ask what I had in the bag. When I told him red licorice, he would ask for a piece. I would barter for a cold *Pepsi* for one piece of licorice and a bag of *Fritos* for the other piece. I went to the store with a nickel in my pocket and came home with eight pieces of candy a cold sixteen-ounce *Pepsi* and a bag of *Fritos*! What was Nelson's problem? His major problem was he lacked any discernment (a secondary one was a neighbor who had little integrity!). I am sure if I approached him today, decades later, and offered the same trades he would laugh at my offer.

C. You will only become **spiritually effective** when you read the Bible well (2 Tim. 3:16–17).

"All Scripture is inspired by God and is profitable for doctrine, reproof, for correction, for instruction in righteousness; that the man of God may be equipped for every good work."

The Bible tells you what's right and true (doctrine), what's false and wrong (reproof), how to get right (correction), and how to stay right (instruction in righteousness). The Bible makes you fully ready for spiritual effectiveness. These days, many people have a Global Positioning System (G.P.S.) device in their cars and phones. The devices are not perfect, but they can be helpful in getting a person to a desired destination. In some ways, the Bible is like a perfect G.P.S.- it informs the reader when he is headed in the desired direction, tells him when he has taken a bad turn, tells him how to get back on track, and then tells him how to stay on course.

Regardless of the roles God puts you in (employee, spouse, ministry leader, parent, etc.) you will be made effective through a study of and commitment to obeying the Word of God.

D. The Bible will **_protect_** you from error and danger (Mark 12:18-27; 2 Peter 3:14-18). The further removed in time we get from the life and ministry of Christ and the writing of the New Testament and the closer we get to the return of Christ for His saints, the more false-doctrine will proliferate (1 Timothy 4:1-3). Considering this, the knowledge of God's Word will protect the believer from false doctrine. The better you know the fundamental, core teachings of God's Word the more protected you will be from heresy.

In addition to these benefits, can you think of others you would receive from a careful study of God's Word?

Now that you are familiar with what Bible study takes and some of its personal benefits, let's become familiar with some key ideas that will help us read the Bible well.

III. Some Core Definitions

Let's define two key terms that are the heart of this course.

A. Hermeneutics

The Greek god Hermes was considered the messenger of the gods. In Greek mythology, his role was to explain to humans what the gods said. He made sure that everyday people understood the gods' messages. The skill of understanding written messages came to be called "hermeneutics." While we do not agree with Greek mythology and beliefs, biblical writers used the Greek words "hermenia" or "hermeneuo" translated as "which means" or "being interpreted" (John 1:38; 9:7; Acts 4:36; 9:36; Heb. 7:2). Simply put, hermeneutics is the ***"principles of interpretation,"*** especially as it relates to the Bible.

B. Inductive Method

Many approaches of studying God's Word are used. They include the "commentary approach" where one merely looks in commentaries to see what others have written and then comes to a conclusion based upon others' interpretations. Perhaps you've heard someone comment, "If you looked at seven commentaries, you'd get eight interpretations." In this approach, the reader consults commentaries and adopts the interpretation he/she likes best, but for no solid reason other than it agrees with their own view(s). Another method is what I'll call the "Holy Spirit will guide me" approach. This approach merely waits for the Spirit to reveal the truth but neglects any work on the part of the student. Yet another approach is the "application approach." In this method, there is no serious study to see what God has said, it involves only looking for applications.

In order to have good results in Bible study, one needs to be like a good cook: follow a great recipe and you will get great results. Haphazardly work through a text of Scripture and disaster will nearly always ensue.

How do we employ our hermeneutics? Our method is known as the inductive method. We work from **_observations_** of the text to **_conclusions/interpretations_** about the text's meaning. For example: You come home from church and discover that your iPad and charger are gone. You begin to look around the room for clues. You find your neighbor's wallet under the coffee table. You know it wasn't there before church because he works nights and you haven't had him over in six months. When you step outside to think about what to do, you hear music coming from your neighbor's back yard. That's odd because he hasn't owned that device before. You look over the fence and there is an iPad on his picnic table. It's the same size and color as yours! When you pick it up, you notice it has your name on a label on the back, right where you put it. Thinking through these observations, you conclude that your neighbor borrowed or stole your iPad and charger. This process is inductive reasoning: to conclude based on facts that you find by observing.

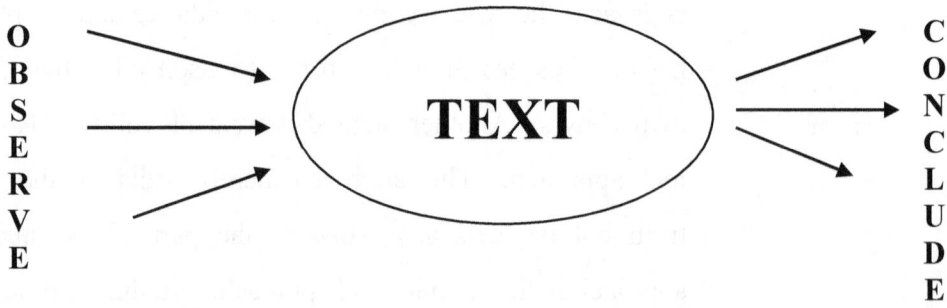

In many ways, studying the Bible is like being a good detective. You look for clues to draw good conclusions. The difference between Bible study and detective work is that God is not trying to hide truth, while most criminals do. The similarity is that just as a good detective cannot ignore any clue a crime scene has to offer, so too the good Bible student must use care to see all the text has to say to draw a good conclusion.

Let me introduce you to two words you will need to be familiar with as a student of the Bible: **"Exegesis"** and **"eisegesis"**. Though they sound a bit similar, their concepts are worlds apart. Both are compound words. To simplify, note the "ex" in exegesis. We get the word "exit" from it. It means "from". When used in Bible study, it means to draw "from" the passage the meaning/interpretation. Exegesis is essentially the inductive method. In eisegesis, note the "eis" prefix. It means "into." Thus, eisegesis is to put into the text words or meanings that are foreign to the text. It is a terrible practice and should be consistently avoided.

Now you are ready to engage in the exciting, profitable, and life changing practice of hermeneutics.

> **Now You Try It #1**
> Review this chapter including the following summary page. Read the next chapter and be prepared to discuss it. Write down any questions your reading generates. Read chapters 1–3 in your textbook. Finally, complete the assignment your teacher gives you and turn it in next class.

Homework Assignment #1: In your own words describe / define what inductive Bible study is. Write it down and be prepared to explain it in class.

Each week, when you complete your homework, make two (2) copies (one to turn in to the professor and one copy to keep and make notes on).

Review / Summary of Chapter 1
DO READ YOU WELL?

I. WHAT IT TAKES TO READ THE BIBLE WELL

    A. Be **regenerated/born again**.

    B. Possess three vital attitudes.
        1. **Desire** for God's truth.
        2. **Dependent** on the Holy Spirit.
        3. **Diligence** in the study of God's Word.

    C. Employ two primary skills.
        1. Read well
        2. Understand what you read

II. SOME BENEFITS OF READING THE BIBLE WELL

    A. You will grow steadily (1 Pet.2:1-2).
    B. You will mature in spiritual ability (Heb. 5:11-14).
    C. You will become spiritually effective (2 Tim. 3:16-17)
    D. You will be protected from spiritual danger and error (2 Pet. 3:14-18)

III. SOME CORE DEFINITIONS

    A. Hermeneutics is the **principles of interpretation**, especially as it relates to the Bible.
    B. Inductive means we work from **observations** of the text to **conclusions** about the meaning of the text.

Chapter 2
THE PRINCIPLE OF PLAIN MEANING

I. THE BIBLE AND NORMAL HUMAN COMMUNICATION

When we communicate with one another, we intend to convey one idea or thought to which others can respond. We view spoken and written language as a reliable means to express that idea or thought. People listen and read with the assumption that what is said is what is meant. For instance, what does a red, octagonal sign with the word STOP in the middle mean? Try getting yourself out of a ticket from a law enforcement officer by saying, "That STOP sign only means slow down and look both ways." If I say to you, "Pass the butter, please," what do I assume that you will do? What do you think I mean? You would not think, "Bill asked for butter, but I know he really wants the green beans." If you passed the green beans I would think you were a bit strange. This idea of plain meaning is one of the basic laws of human communication.

The Bible is written for people to understand and obey. Because people communicate to be understood, God wrote the Bible following the ***principles*** of written communication. Put another way, God understands how we communicate, and He stooped to our level of communication, so He would be understood. He expects us to read the Bible using those principles. When we read Scripture according to the principles of human communication, we understand it. Let's explore this principle.

II. THE PRINCIPLE OF PLAIN MEANING

This concept is our first principle of hermeneutics. What do we mean by the principle of plain meaning? The principle of plain meaning teaches us several things.

    A.   Take the words at face value.

According to the principle of plain meaning, we accept the normal, usual meaning of words and terms, including figures of speech. An example of the principle of plain meaning is found in **_Matthew 19:3-6_**. There, Jesus took the plain meaning of the words of Genesis 1 and 2, "In the beginning..." and built His teaching about marriage on them. To put it another way, when Jesus read the words, "In the beginning..." in Genesis 1:1, He believed that they meant just that, in the beginning, not after millions or billions of years of time. We should take the Bible's words at face value too.

When you interpret the Bible the way Jesus did, you will never go wrong. This concept is just the first of several truths we will discover in this course concerning how Jesus interpreted the Bible.

    B. There is only one meaning.

In human language, a statement normally has only one meaning. When a person speaks, he intends his words to convey one idea. He does not intend one statement to have several different meanings. Unless the communicator says there is a second intended meaning, his statement is taken to have only one meaning. Likewise, a Bible passage has only one correct interpretation where there may be several good applications. Even an idiom, symbol, figure of speech, poetry or prophecy conveys only one idea at a time.

It is common for students to believe that there are several interpretations to any given passage of Scripture. Often, they will raise an objection to this concept and say, "There are many interpretations to a passage. It means one thing today and when I read it later it means a completely different thing." My response? "The passage only ever has one interpretation." What changes is NOT the interpretation, but one's understanding of the meaning. When I was twenty-one years old, one week after my college graduation, I stood before family, friends, a pastor and God and I made a vow, "For better or worse, richer or poorer, in sickness and in health 'till death do us part." Those words' meanings have not changed. What has changed is my understanding of them. When I was 21 years old, I only knew health and better; I figured poorer would always be true! Now I understand more fully the speed bumps of a relationship and the sickness that most twenty-one-year old people never think about. The meaning of the vows didn't change. It was my understanding from experience that has caused them to take on a fuller meaning.

C. The meaning is God's message.

Since the words of Scripture at face value have only one correct meaning, we seek that meaning. The meaning the author intended to relate is in the text. The author's meaning is God's message. We do not look for what it means to us. We seek the meaning the author intended. This concept is also called literal interpretation or authorial intent.

III. COMMON MISTAKES WHEN READING THE BIBLE

Many people fail to honor the principle of plain meaning. Instead, they often practice three common fallacies.

A. They practice what is called *spiritualizing* the text.

This practice looks for hidden meanings that are not clearly indicated by the writer and are not consistent with the plain, ordinary use of language.

Failure to take a passage literally can result in all sorts of fanciful interpretations. This practice became popular in the fourth century (***Augustine*** popularized this method and it has become the leading method of the church today).

For example, read the story of Genesis 24. It tells how Abraham provided a godly wife for Isaac in the land of promise. Very often though, people make it into an allegory and find "spiritual" meaning in it. For instance, Abraham represents God the Father, Isaac represents Jesus, and Eleazar is the Holy Spirit. Rebekah is a picture of the church, and the chapter is all about how God provides a bride for Jesus! Ask yourself two questions about this interpretation. One, is that what the ***original readers*** of Genesis would have understood? Imagine that Moses, the human author of Genesis, handed you the original writing of this passage fourteen centuries before Christ's birth. If you were the first reader, would you have thought it was a story about God the Father looking for a bride for His Son, Jesus, and sending the Holy Spirit to find her? Two, is that what the ***words say at face value***? Of course, the answer on both accounts is a resounding NO!

Avoid spiritualizing at all costs. God wants to communicate truth. He has chosen to reveal Himself in plain words.

B. People often *import* ideas into a passage.

An import is something that is foreign; it comes from another place/ country. While it may not be bad for an economy to import items from abroad, it is disastrous in Bible Study. At times people have an idea they want to talk about or to confirm. The idea may be true, it may even be biblical, but that truth is not the message of the text. Instead of letting the text speak for itself, they read their idea into the passage. This concept is called **eisegesis**.

Perhaps a church leader is dead set against divorce. As he teaches through Matthew, he comes to chapter 19. He teaches that Matthew 19:3-12 prohibits divorce for any reason. That is his conclusion, even though Jesus gave an acceptable reason for divorce in verse 9. Always let the passage speak for itself.

C. People often *conclude* without reading the passage.

Have you ever heard or said, "Money is the root of all evil" or "God helps those who help themselves" or "God wants you to prosper"? These are common statements heard in church, but not one of them is a biblical statement. Each is half-truth based on a failure to completely read the text. Be very careful that you fully read a passage before you conclude what it means. This practice can be particularly difficult for those who have heard sermons for many years. Past exposure to the Scriptures can lead the reader to assume he/she already knows what a particular passage teaches. In fact, in some ways, a new convert has an advantage over the older saint here. The new believer has fewer preconceived ideas about any text, while the older believer often has his mind made up.

IV. CHECKING YOUR CONCLUSIONS

How can we check our understanding? Here are five ways to see if you have properly understood the text.

A. First, the ***most obvious*** meaning is usually the correct meaning. The usual and most natural sense of a word or passage should be considered correct unless the context demands otherwise. Any passage should be understood literally unless the literal sense makes no sense. An oft-quoted, helpful guideline is: "If the literal sense makes good sense, seek no other sense, lest it result in nonsense."

Those who study test taking, have discovered that when a student takes a test, upon seeing a question, their first response is often the correct response. This is often true in Bible study too.

B. Second, the correct meaning will always be ***consistent*** with the context and the rest of the Bible. For example, although strange to our experience, it makes sense to interpret Isaiah 11:6 literally. *"And the wolf shall dwell with the lamb..."* Because we know the Bible teaches a coming earthly kingdom of Jesus, and because this passage refers to that kingdom, it makes great sense that even the animals will be at peace with one another when Jesus establishes His Kingdom. You've never seen a wolf and a lamb be at peace with each other, so why would this be consistent with the Word of God? Because the King, who created all things, will one day rule the earth and He made animals to be at peace in the Garden of Eden, it is perfectly consistent with those truths to believe the wolf and lamb will be at peace with each other when He reigns.

C. **Third, the meaning will be *logical*.** The concept presented in the passage may be something beyond normal human ability (such as Jesus walking on water), but it is logical in light of all the facts you collect from the text. For example, you cannot walk on water, but it is a logical conclusion to draw from the Bible regarding Jesus. Since you also know He is Creator of all things, His walking on water is logical interpretation. This truth is a bit like the previous point. In the eighteenth century, liberal theologians in Germany influenced much of the world. They denied the miraculous (their worldview did not allow for the supernatural) and thus had to "reinterpret" miracles in Scripture. These theologians said that Jesus did not walk on water (remember, they deny the miraculous). What actually happened was that He knew the Sea of Galilee so well He knew where there were tree stumps submerged just below the water's surface, and He walked on them. At this point one doesn't know whether to laugh or cry! Given what we know about Jesus in the rest of Scripture since He created the entire universe in six days, walking on water is no longer seen as difficult. As Creator of all things, how hard would it be for Him to walk on water He created? This truth is the logical conclusion to reach about the passage.

D. Fourth, when a word or passage appears to have more than one meaning, the ***simplest understanding*** should be chosen. This principle should govern the interpreter because God intends for her to understand His message. Remember God revealed His Word to ordinary people in an agricultural society. If it takes a computer or advanced degrees to explain and/or understand it, it probably is not a good interpretation.

E. Check a good ***commentary***, but only check them after you have finished your own work. **Note**: This is the **last** step, not the first. Usually, it is the first place a person turns, when it should be the last place. When a commentary is referred to first, little or nothing is learned by the student other than what the writer of the commentary believes. An appendix of good commentaries is provided.

> **Now You Try It #2**
>
> Review this chapter including the following summary page and be ready for a quiz over it next class. Read the next chapter in *Digging Deeper* and be prepared to discuss it. Write down any questions your reading generates. Read chapters 7, 30-31, 33-34 in *Living by the Book*. Finally, complete the assignment your teacher gives you and turn it in next class.

Homework Assignment #2 Remember to make two copies of your work.

1. Answer this question from Chapter 7 in *Living by the Book:* How could I learn to read better?

2. What are the five contexts Hendricks writes about in *Living by the Book*?

Review / Summary of Chapter 2
THE PRINCIPLE OF PLAIN MEANING

I. The Bible and Normal Human Communication
The Bible is written within and follows the principles of normal human communication. Its intent is to be understood and obeyed.

II. The Principle of Plain Meaning
    A. Take the words at **face value**.
    B. A text has only **one meaning**.
    C. The meaning of the text is **God's message**.

III. Common Mistakes when Reading the Bible
    A. People often **spiritualize** the text–find a hidden meaning in the Word or more "spiritual" interpretation of the text.
    B. People often **import** ideas into a passage–missing the truth of the text.
    C. People often **conclude** without reading the passage.

IV. Checking your Conclusions
    A. The **most obvious** meaning is usually the correct meaning. "If the literal sense makes good sense, seek no other sense, lest it result in nonsense."
    B. The correct meaning will always be consistent with the **context** and the rest of the Bible.
    C. The meaning will be **logical**
    D. When a word or passage appears to have more than one meaning, the **simplest** understanding should be chosen.
    E. Check good commentaries, but only check them **after** you have finished your own work.

Chapter 3
THE PRINCIPLE OF CONTEXT pt. 1

Context is key. Indeed, we might even say that context is king! Without context, we cannot know the meaning of words, sentences, or any written or verbal communication. Let me explain, unless a word is put into the context of a sentence, it only has possible meanings, but not a specific one. Can you list five ways the word "trunk" is used?

    example: "nose" of an elephant

    _____

    _____

    _____

    _____

So, what does the word "trunk" mean? Context is crucial, isn't it? You have at least five possible choices. The correct answer is, "It depends upon the context." Another good response would be, "It only has a range of possible meanings," until or unless put into a sentence or paragraph, it means nothing.

I. The Principle of Context Described and Illustrated

The principle of context teaches us that a passage's meaning can be found by examining the environment in which it rests. Another way to state it is that we understand a text in light of its setting.

What is that environment or setting in which every text rests? Context is the **literary**, **theological**, **historical**, and **book** setting of a word, sentence, or paragraph that always determines its meaning. Literary context deals with the type of literature you are reading and how it influences meaning. Theological context deals with how God related to people in the time of the passage you are reading. Historical context refers to the culture and circumstances when the passage was written. Finally, book context refers to the relationships between the theme, purpose and structure of the book.

One biblical example of the principle of context is **Luke 20:27-40**. Jesus employed it when the Sadducees confronted him over his belief in the resurrection. He referred to the historical context of Exodus 3 when He quoted Ex. 3:6, 15. **Jesus always observed the principle of context, and so should we**. Imagine the context as a series of boxes surrounding the text you are interpreting. Always start with the outside and work into the text as you summarize the context.

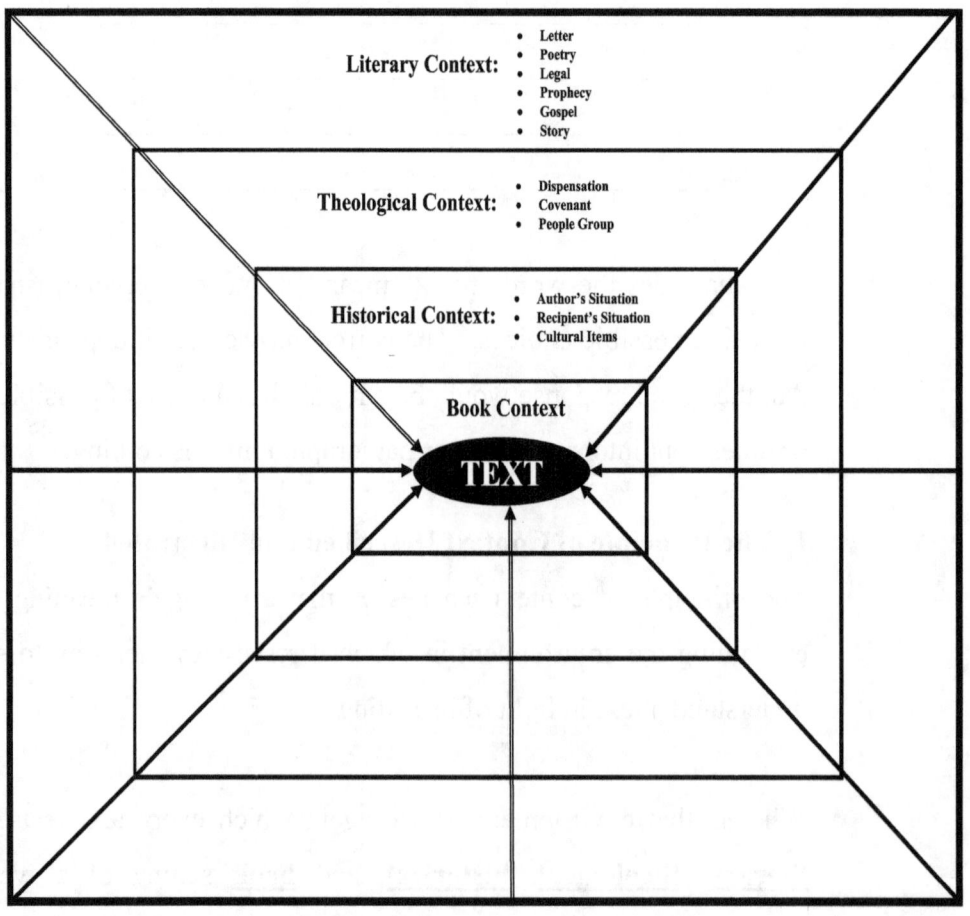

II. The Literary Context

The type of literature we read determines how we read it. For instance, you read a comic book differently than you do a mobile phone contract. Why? You read poetry differently than you do a letter from home. Why? Although you read the various literatures differently, you still read them for their literal meaning, don't you? You must learn to do the same with Scripture.

The sixty-six books of the Bible consist of many different literary types. Literary context deals with the type of literature, also known as genre. Awareness of the type of literature you are reading helps when you overview a book and when you analyze individual texts. It helps you see paragraphs and verses in light of the whole book. It protects you from taking them out of context and from reading more out of a text than you should.

For now, determine whether a book is **poetry**, **letter/epistle**, **gospel**, **legal**, **prophecy**, or **narrative** when you read it. When determining the literary context, understand that you are "painting with a broad brush." You are stating a general observation on the type of literature you are considering, yet you may well note that the book contains brief sections of other types of literature (e.g., the book may be a letter but contain a few verses of prophecy).

III. The Theological Context

From the beginning of the Bible (Genesis 1:26-28) to the end (Revelation 22:3-5), the theme of scripture is a kingdom. More specifically, God's kingdom. A kingdom ruled by God would be called a theocracy. In His theocracy, God delegated authority to rule to people (Adam and Eve).
Sometime after their creation and God's delegation, Adam and Eve rebelled against God and plunged mankind into a state of rebellion. As rebels against their Creator, they were no longer fit to rule for Him. In grace, God worked to restore fallen humanity. The rest of scripture is the record of God's work to restore His kingdom and ultimately have His own Son, Jesus, rule eternally.

Three key truths to understanding the theological context of any passage of scripture are: dispensation, covenant, and people group. Put in question form: What dispensation does the passage being considered fall into? What covenant are the people addressed under? Finally, what group of people are being addressed in the passage? Let's consider each.

A. Know the *dispensational* context

Through history, God exercises His rule through different means at different times. The Bible refers to these times of God's rule as **_dispensations_**. A dispensation is merely a period of time. The word technically means, "household management." It is how God manages/administers/rules His "household"/creation. The verses below detail more about this concept. Suffice it to say there are two dispensation/periods of time that dominate most of the pages of the Bible. The **law** was given to Israel in Exodus 19 through the New Testament Gospels. Remember when Jesus said he was about to institute a new covenant and with it a new dispensation? The second major dispensation, the **church** (sometimes referred to as "grace"), began at Pentecost (Acts 2) and essentially runs through most of the rest of the New Testament. Sometimes a text will be in one dispensation but will speak of future or past dispensations. Accurate interpretation and application demand that we understand the dispensational context of every text we study. Notice the following verses:

- "…with a view to an **_administration_** suitable to the fullness of the times, *that is*, the summing up of all things in Christ, things in the heavens and things on the earth. In Him" (Eph 1:10).

- "…if indeed you have heard of the **_stewardship_** of God's grace which was given to me for you and to bring to light what is the **_administration_** of the mystery which for ages has been hidden in God who created all things;" (Eph 3:2, 9).

- "Why the _**Law**_ then? It was _**added**_ because of transgressions, having been ordained through angels by the agency of a mediator, until the seed would come to whom the promise had been made" (Gal 3:19).

Let me attempt to illustrate this concept from the history of the United States using our own constitution. The eighteenth amendment to the U.S. constitution was passed in 1920 and prohibited the sale, distribution, and consumption of all alcoholic beverages in the United States (known as Prohibition). Later in 1933, the twenty-first amendment was passed which overturned the previous prohibition on alcohol. These two amendments represent two "dispensations", or periods, in U.S. history. During one period (dispensation) it was illegal to sell, possess, or purchase alcohol. During the second, it was legally permissible.

Another historical reality helps illustrate this principle. In the United States in the 1960's, the legal voting age was 21 years. During the Vietnam War era, many young men and women protested, stating the U.S. government considered them adults by sending them to war but would not let them vote. In 1971, the 26th amendment was passed giving 18-year-old citizens the right to register to vote. Prior to 1971 it was illegal for all citizens of the United States under the age of 21 to vote but legal and even encouraged after that time for those who were 18 years old or older and who were registered to vote.

Both historical events demonstrate the principle of dispensations. They are merely an era, a time period. What occurs during that period? We often speak of a president's time in office as his administration. During the four, or perhaps eight, years he was in office how did he manage the country?

On a personal note, every person's life has different dispensations. Each of us had a time when we were confined, very comfortably, in our mother's womb. Then we had childhood. Most of us received a driver's license (freedom!) at age 16. Many got married in their 20's and many have children. These are distinct periods in a person life and to fail to recognize them would be a failure to understand life (eighteen-year old adults don't still take naps or go to bed at 8:00 PM and three-year old toddlers can't legally drive a car).

Consider the following verses concerning the principle of dispensations:
- *Evangelism*: Matthew 10:6 (compare Matthew 28:19, 20; Acts 1:8)
- *Diet*: Genesis 1:29; 9:3, 4; Lev 11:3, 10; 1 Tim 4:4
- *Clothing*: Leviticus 19:19
- *Agriculture*: Leviticus 25:4
- *Punishment of wayward child:* Deuteronomy 21:18-21

B. Know the *covenant* context

You also need to be aware of the covenant that was in place when your text was written. Dispensations are periods of time while covenants express the rules/conditions in that era/time. For our purposes, a *covenant is an agreement between God and man*. While there are several covenants in the Bible, two that are especially significant. That is why the Bible is divided into two parts: The Old Testament (testament is another word for covenant) and the New Testament (covenant). There are also two kinds of covenants: conditional and unconditional. Though the words "conditional" or "unconditional" are not used in the covenants, the language clearly states what sort of covenant it is. Conditional covenants use language such as "if you...then I..." Unconditional covenants merely say, "I will..." Covenants detail how God relates to people of that dispensation. Today, we will not be stoned for picking up sticks on the Sabbath, nor are we required to worship on the Sabbath. Why not? Because God changed the covenant; we are ruled by grace rather than law (Rom. 6:14).

In the Mosaic Covenant (the law given through Moses to Israel), many responsibilities were placed upon Israel. God expected obedience and promised blessings for such obedience. Conversely, He promised punishment upon His people if they fail to follow obediently. The Mosaic Covenant covers most of the Bible from Exodus 20 through the end of the four Gospels. The New Covenant is in effect from Acts 2 through Revelation 19.

In the New Covenant, which was instituted after the death of Jesus, all believers were/are given the permanent indwelling of the Holy Spirit and empowered to serve God faithfully (Jer. 31:31-34; Matt. 26:28; Mark 14:22-25).

To meld the concepts of dispensation and covenant, simply ask what was the covenant (regulations or agreement) in place at the time (era, dispensation) of the passage being written?

In many states, obtaining a driver's license is a process. The potential driver must pass a written test and be of a minimum age. Upon passing the test, the driver receives a "permit." Certain rules apply to the driver (usually they include having a parent or guardian present in the front seat). The newly minted driver must have the permit for a minimal amount of time (often a year). That arrangement is a good illustration of dispensations (a period of time-how long the driver will be in this arrangement) and covenants (what rules apply during that period). Not every person is under every covenant. Some covenants only apply to certain people. Others might apply to all people, but for only a period of time that has past or is future.

C. Know the *people* context

Finally, to clarify the theological context, determine the people group addressed in the passage. God has distinct purposes, times, and messages for three different people groups throughout history. According to 1 Cor. 10:32, they are the **_Jew_**, the **_Gentile_** (non-Jew), and the **_church_** (believers in Jesus, regardless of ethnicity, from Pentecost until the rapture). Never confuse the people groups. In the Old Testament one was either a Jew or Gentile, but all were born lost in sin. Though lost, the Jew had a distinct advantage over the Gentile, because he knew of the Creator God, the sacrificial system, the promise of a Redeemer, etc. The Gentile did not have God's special revelation. It is therefore critical to determine who is being addressed in the text: Are they Jew, Gentile or Church? Never confuse Israel and the church. God made some very specific and eternal promises to

Israel that almost exclusively do not apply to the church. Ask of the text: are the people addressed believers or unbelievers? Let the text provide your answer.

When I was young my family would travel to the state of Iowa, where our roots and many family members were. In the 1970's in Iowa, a young person could get a permit to drive a car at the age of 14. Some of my cousins had permits to drive but I did not. The law in Oklahoma (where I lived) did not allow this arrangement until age $15^{1/2}$. The people group my cousins were in was Iowans while I was an Oklahoman. I was from a different people group therefore I was under a different set of regulations.

What people group was the text you are studying written to? Observing and understanding this concept will aid greatly in your interpretation of the scriptures. For example, consider the following:

Identify the people group for each of the following passages:

- 2 Chronicles 7:14
- Exodus 22:18
- Deuteronomy 6:12
- Joshua 1:4

While all of scripture was written **for us** (for our edification/learning), it was not all written directly **to us**.

OVERVIEW OF COVENANTS/DISPENSATIONS

Dispensation	Texts	People Ruled	Time Frame	Covenant
Promise	Gen. 1 – Exod. 18	All Men	Past / Present / Future	Abrahamic
Law	Exod. 19 - Acts 1	Israel	Past	Mosaic
Grace	Acts 2 - Rev. 3	Church	Present	New
Kingdom	Rev. 4 – 22	All Men	Future	Abrahamic

To summarize: theological context consists of (1) the dispensation (a period of time), (2) covenant (the agreement between God and people), and (3) the people group (Jew, Gentile or Church) addressed in the text. Always determine the theological context.

Review:

I. The Principle of Context Described and Illustrated
   A. A passage derives its meaning from the **environment** in which it rests. Another way to state it is that we understand a text in light of its **setting**.

   B. Context is the **literary**, **theological**, historical, and book setting of a word, sentence, or paragraph that always determines its meaning.

II. Determine the Literary Context
   A. Literary context deals with the type of literature we read.

   B. Is it poetry, letter, gospel, prophecy or narrative?

III. Determine the Theological Context
   A. God has expressed His rule through different people at different times.
   B. What is the dispensation?
   C. What is the covenant?
   D. What is the people group context: Jew, Gentile or Church?

NOW YOUR TRY #3

Read chapters 4-6 in *Living by the Book.* In addition, complete the following.

Homework:

1. What is the Literary context for each of the following books?

   A. Philippians: _____

   B. Matthew: _____

   C. Psalms: _____

   D. Genesis: _____

2. Using the chart on page 50, list the **_dispensation, covenant, AND people group_** for each of the books of the Bible below:

	Dispensation	Covenant	People group
Leviticus			
Isaiah			
Ephesians			
Colossians			

Chapter 4
PRINCIPLE OF CONTEXT pt. 2

Context is so important we cannot cover it in one lesson. We return to the topic again in this chapter. We've already discovered that there is literary context and theological context. What else is there? Next, we come to historical context. Do you remember the earlier context box chart? To keep it fresh in our minds, here it is again:

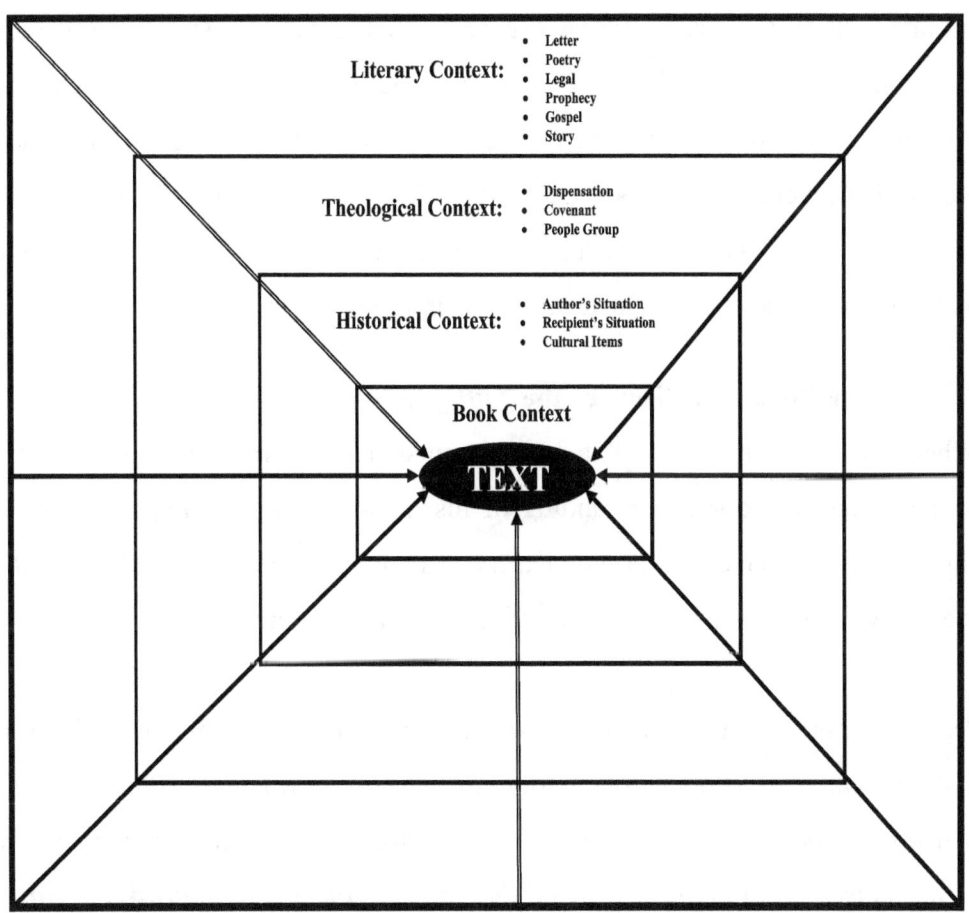

God revealed the Scriptures progressively (step by step) through historical situations (Heb 1:1-3; John 16:12, 13). To be an excellent student of the Bible, you must understand the role the historical setting played in shaping the message of a passage. For instance, assume you write a letter today. In the letter, you mention you had a "great time in your Caravan interfacing with your friend Susan and that you "upgraded you RAM by 80 gigs" and that you "outsourced your network maintenance". You "snail mail" the letter but it gets lost and never arrives to the addressee. In fact, it remains lost and unread for 800 years before an archeologist finds it. How do you suppose a world with no RAM, no Caravans, and no outsourcing would understand what you wrote? In our culture RAM is a computer term referring to "Random Access Memory", but in Abraham's day it was an animal. For us, a Caravan is a Dodge product. In Joseph's day, it was a string of camels crossing a desert.

Another way to understand the importance of this principle is suppose a person came to the United States from a foreign country and had been "living under a rock" their entire life. He decides to study and even write a book about the greatness of the United States. If he were to write about the past 80+ years and not understand the significance of December 7, 1941 (Pearl Harbor) or September 11, 2001 (World Trade Center) then he would not understand significant events in today's culture.

A. **Read the Book and Discover the *Author's Situation*.**

Where the author was, what his circumstances were, and why he wrote add tremendously to your understanding of his message. For example, Jonah boarded a ship to flee from God. When you learn that Israelites were greatly afraid of the sea and sea travel, you learn about his motivation to get away from God.

As an example, when you read through the book of Philippians you will soon discover that Paul was in prison when he wrote this letter: "*For it is only right for me to feel this way about you all, because I have you in my heart, since both in my imprisonment and in the defense and confirmation of the gospel, you all are partakers with me* (Phil. 1:7)." When you read through Philippians you discover that Paul wrote extensively about joy. It is one thing to tell others to be joyful when you are on a nice beach sipping a cold iced tea, quite another to encourage them to be joyful, as you intend to be, from prison.

Let's practice this principle in class. From Ephesians chapter 1, jot down five (5) observations about the author's situation. Be sure to include chapter and verse for each observation.

1. _____
2. _____
3. _____
4. _____
5. _____

B. Read the Book and Discover the *Recipient's Situation*.

You should also learn as much about the recipients as you can. As with the author's situation, there will be much insight within the book itself. Discover as much as you can about their circumstances, challenges, opportunities, and culture. Again, in the book of Philippians, we read, *"And you yourselves also know, Philippians, that at the first preaching of the gospel, after I departed from Macedonia, no church shared with me in the matter of giving and receiving but you alone"* (Phil. 4:15). From this verse we know the church in Philippi was the only church who gave to support Paul's ministry financially. The following verse says, *"For even in Thessalonica you sent a gift more than once for my needs"* (Phil. 4:16). They were not a "one and done" congregation, moved to action once and then on to forgetfulness. They gave on multiple occasions. Observing truths like these will help enlighten your understanding of God's Word.

Let's practice this principle in class. Again, from Ephesians chapter, 1 jot down five (5) observations about the recipient's situation. Be sure to include chapter and verse for each observation.

1. _____
2. _____
3. _____
4. _____
5. _____

C. Read the Book and note any <u>*Cultural items*</u> you don't understand.

You will often find things mentioned in Scripture that are foreign to your culture and experience. For instance, why would God prohibit boiling a baby goat in its mother's milk? Or, why was Jesus wrapped in swaddling clothes? How was his body prepared for burial and what did the disciples see when they found his grave clothes? Knowing the historical and cultural setting in which the text was written is critical to good understanding.

For example, as you read through Philippians you come across terms like:
- praetorian guard (1:13)
- bond-servants (1:1)

Jot down each cultural item you do not understand. Your list will serve as a reminder that you will want to discover what these terms mean at a future time.

A note of caution: at this point only <u>write down</u> what you don't understand, culturally, do not put down your Bible to seek an answer just yet. If you do you might get sidetracked and/or immersed in other things rather than observing the text.

D. Use Other Tools to Aid Your Discovery

Needing to learn about the culture and background is one thing. Doing it is another! Where can you go to learn about the historical setting of a passage or book? There are several helpful places to look.

Always start with the text itself. Many times, it will explain cultural items. The book as a whole will tell you almost everything you need to know about the author and the recipient's circumstances. You must train yourself to look and see.

Compare other books by or about the same author. For example, the story of Paul's missionary ministry in Philippi (Acts 16:11-40) presents background information for a study of his letter to the Philippians. Likewise, the historical books of the Old Testament provide the historical background of the prophets (e.g. compare Samuel with Kings and Chronicles). In the Gospels, read the three that you are not studying to get a better sense of the one gospel you are considering (a resource called *A Harmony of the Gospels* is very helpful here).

Notes in Study Bibles are helpful in locating the historical background of a particular passage. Some helpful Bible Study tools that provide such information on Bible culture are:

- William L. Coleman, **Today's Handbook of Bible Times and Customs** (Minneapolis: Bethany House, 1984)

- James I. Packer, Merrill C. Tenney and William White, eds., **The Bible Almanac** (Nashville: Thomas Nelson, 1980)

-J.A. Thompson, **Handbook of Life in Bible Times** (Downers Grove: IVP, 1986)

- Ralph Gower, **The New Manners and Customs of Bible Times** (Chicago: Moody, 1986)

- Merrill F. Unger, **The Unger's Bible Dictionary** (Chicago: Moody Press, 1978)

- Merrill C. Tenney, ed., **The Zondervan Pictorial Encyclopedia of the Bible** (Grand Rapids, Zondervan, 1976).

In recent times, many serious Bible students have purchased the *Logos Bible Software* package. There are many valuable resources available in that software, including many of the above-mentioned volumes.

Remember that we are separated from the world of the Bible by thousands of years. Always place a passage in its context. Start with the literary type. Then determine the theological context. Next, clarify the historical setting. Put your feet in their sandals. Feel their challenges. Think through their worldview. As you do, the Scriptures will come to life.

REVIEW:

Determine the Historical Context
A. Read the book and discover the author's situation.
B. Read the book and discover the recipient's situation
C. Read the book and note any cultural items you don't understand
D. Use other books to aid your discovery.

> **Now You Try It #4**
>
> Review this chapter including the following summary page. Read the next chapter in *Digging Deeper* and be prepared to discuss it. Write down any questions your reading generates. Read chapters 8, 11 and 12 in *Living by the Book*. Finally, complete the assignment your teacher gives you and turn it in next class.

Homework Assignment #4 Again, don't forget to create two (2) copies of your homework, one to turn in and one to keep and take notes on.

1. List at least 15 observations of author's situation (chapter and verse).
   1. (e.g. 1. Paul was in prison. Phil 1:7)

   2.

   3.

   4.

   5.

   6.

   7.

   8.

   9.

   10.

   11.

   12.

   13.

   14.

   15.

*Homework continued on next page

2. List at least 15 observations of readers' situation (chapter and verse).
   - (e.g. 1. The believers at Philippi gave to support Paul's ministry financially. Phil. 4:15)

   1.

   2.

   3.

   4.

   5.

   6.

   7.

   8.

   9.

   10.

   11.

   12.

   13.

   14.

   15.

Chapter 5
THE PRINCIPLE OF CONTEXT, pt. 3

Our last two studies introduced the principle of context. We began by looking for the literary and theological context. Then we considered the historical context of the book. Now let's move ahead and explore the most crucial level of the context – **the book context**. Here you want to grasp how the passage you are reading fits into the book itself. For our sake, we will assume your passage is a paragraph and that is the primary unit of thought. There is much more to book context than what we can practice in this course. Another course in hermeneutics will build on the

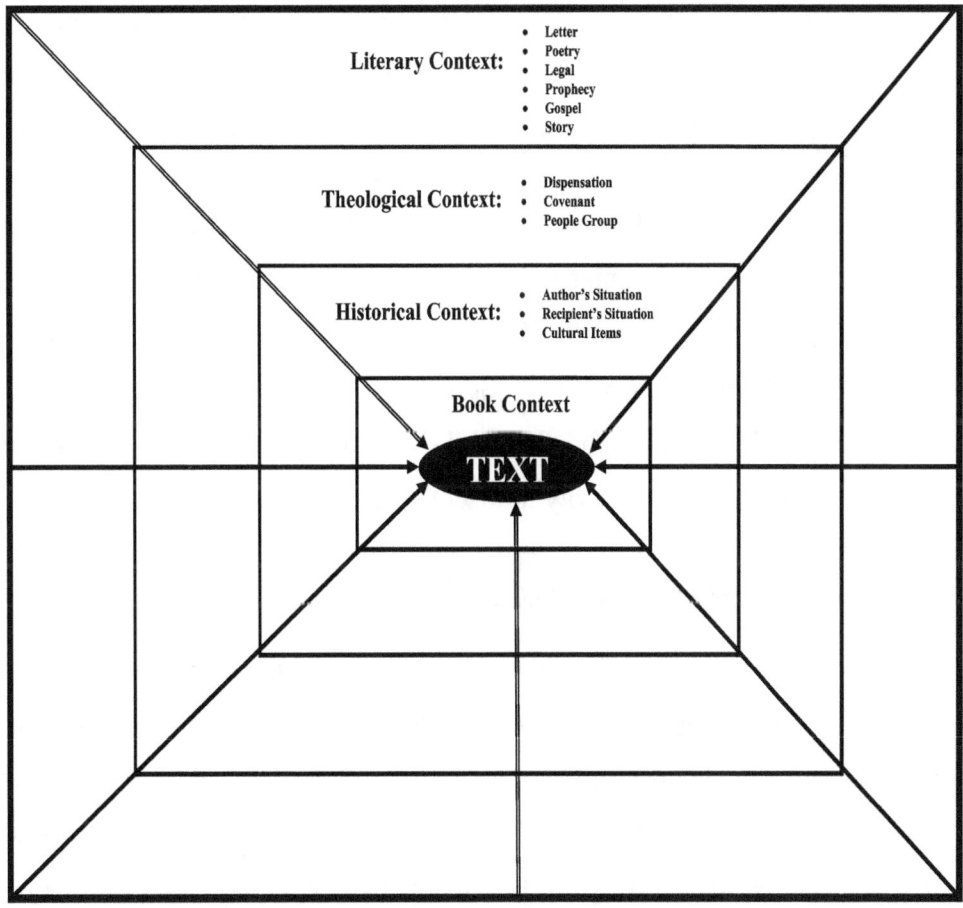

foundations laid in this course.

I. Discover the *Overall* Context

A. Discover the book ***theme***. The theme is what the book is about. Every book has one major theme – the big idea the book is about. You must **_read_** and **_re-read_** the book, constantly asking "What is this about?" to discern the theme.

One of my favorite secular authors is John Grisham. The first book of his, that I read, was *The Testament*. I read it while on a short-term mission trip to Mongolia. Suppose I was sitting next to a stranger on a plane, reading a Grisham book and the stranger asked about the book and my admiration of Grisham's writing. The stranger asks, "Bill, what is your favorite Grisham book?" I respond with, "*The Testament* was my first Grisham book and still my favorite." The stranger responds, "What was it about?" Wouldn't it seem odd to you if I said, "I don't know"? Yet often believers read specific books of the Bible multiple times and yet have no idea what the theme of the book is. Keep reading until you are confident you can summarize the theme of the book in a concise manner.

B. Discover the book ***purpose***. Every book of the Bible also has a unique intent or reason for being written. Each book has one main goal. To determine the purpose of the Bible book being studied is essential. Read and reread it asking, "Why was this written?" Sometimes the purpose is ***stated*** within the book itself, (cf. John 20:31 and Rev. 1:1-3). Most of the time, you must read through the entire book repeatedly to discover the purpose.

II. Discover the *Immediate* Context

A. Understand the theme of the ***paragraph*** immediately before and after your text. Paragraphs are the primary unit of thought and you must grasp their big idea. The paragraph you are studying will be in relationship to at least the preceding and following paragraphs. Quite often, understanding those paragraphs allows you to grasp correctly the meaning of the one you are looking at. Pay careful attention to each one. You should be able to write down the main point of each paragraph in a sentence of no more than eight words. Remember that the theme is what the paragraph is about. When you read ask, "What are the repeated ideas?" or "What words are repeated?" or "What is the topic sentence about?" Discover the answer to these questions for the paragraph ***before*** and the paragraph ***after*** the one you are studying. The exception to this practice is if you are studying the first or last paragraph of the book.

B. State the theme of the paragraph you are developing. Do this by completing four steps.

1. ***Re-read*** your paragraph several times. You may or may not understand everything it says, but what seems to be the big idea? What's the one main point the paragraph is about? Keep that in mind and go to the next step.

2. Think about how your ***paragraph*** relates to the one preceding. Does it ***develop***, **explain**, **illustrate,** or **apply** the preceding? Does it **change subjects**, **compare,** or **conclude**?

3. How does your paragraph relate to the one ***following***? Does either one develop, explain, illustrate, or apply the other? Do they change subjects, compare, or conclude?

4. Now, thinking through all you discovered, ***summarize*** the main point of your paragraph in a sentence of fewer than eight words.

For example, read Philippians 2:1-30. Understanding the preceding and following paragraph helps us clarify this. Fill in the blocks below with your one sentence summary of the message of each paragraph.

Philippians 2:1-11

Philippians 2:12-18

Philippians 2:19-30

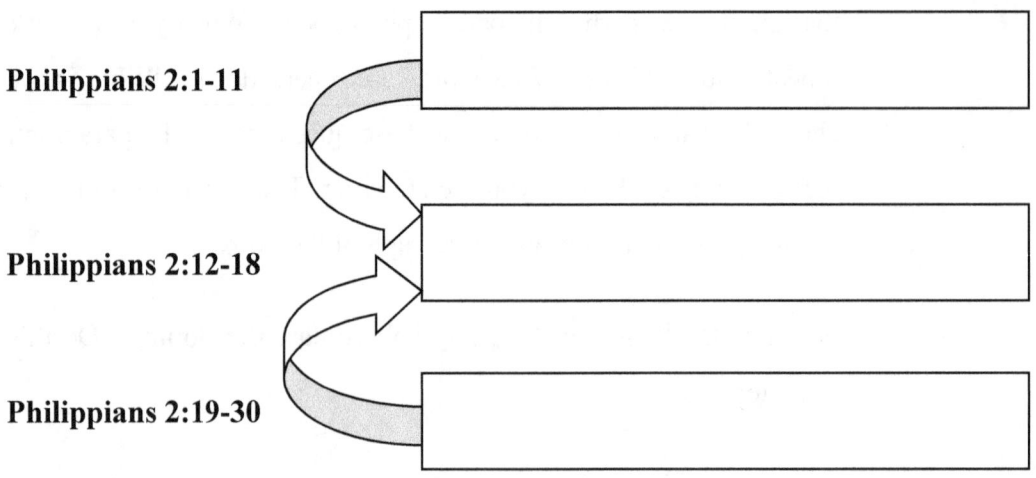

This is one example from one chapter of the book of Philippians. How would a student do this for an entire book of the Bible? Let's take a quick look at the book of Ephesians as an example.

Most seasoned students of the Bible, as they study the book of Ephesians, believe the book divides into three main sections in addition to the introduction and conclusion. How do they arrive at that and how can major sections of the book be found?

Salutation/introduction 1:1,2

1. WEALTH OF THE BELIEVER   1:3-3:21
   - Read carefully the following verses and note the words in each that refer to wealth/riches, etc. – 1:7, 18; 2:4, 7; 3:8, 16. Do you see where the concept comes from?

2. WALK OF THE BELIEVER 4:1-6:9
   - Read carefully the following verses and note the words in each that refer to the walk/living of the believer – 4:1, 17; 5:2, 8, 15

3. WARFARE OF THE BELIEVER 6:10-20
4. CONCLUSION/FINAL THOUGHTS 6:21-24

If one were to outline the entire book, what would that look like? Use the above outline with its major themes as our scaffold to build on. Summarize each paragraph below in eight words or less. **NOTE**: *Your personal outline may not match this one.*

1. WEALTH OF THE BELIEVER 1:3-3:21

    A. _____ 1:3-4

    B. _____ 1:5-13

    C. _____ 1:13-14

    D. _____ 1:15-23

    E. _____ 2:1-10

    F. _____ 2:11-22

    G. _____ 3:1-13

    H. _____ 3:14-21

2. WALK OF THE BELIEVER 4:1-6:9

    A. _____ 4:1-6

    B. _____ 4:7-16

    C. _____ 4:17-32

    D. _____ 5:1-17

    E. _____ 5:18-21

    F. _____ 5:22-6:4

    G. _____ 6:5-9

3. WARFARE OF THE BELIEVER 6:10-20

    A. _____ 6:10-12

    B. _____ 6:13-20

C. Write down anything that confuses you or is unclear. You will clarify it later. The consideration of context is extremely important in Bible study. To adhere faithfully to context expresses your **_respect_** for the authority of Scripture. Context is the most important means we have to determine meaning. The Bible is a 66-book collection that's put together one book at a time. Each book has its own theme and purpose. To understand the Bible, employ the principle of context.

> **Now You Try It #5**
>
> Review this chapter including the following summary page. Read the next chapter in *Digging Deeper* and be prepared to discuss it. Write down any questions your reading generates. Read chapters 15 and 35 in *Living by the Book*. Finally, complete the assignment your teacher gives you and turn it in next class.

Homework Assignment #5

Write your answers to the following questions down and come to class prepared to discuss them.

From Chapter 15 of *Living by the Book*:

1. What is purposeful reading as Hendricks describes it in *Living by the Book*?

From Chapter 35 of *Living by the Book*:

2. What does Hendricks suggest is the nature of doing a word study?

Book Outline: Philippians

1. Outline the **entire** book of Philippians into paragraphs using our exercise in class through the book of Ephesian or pages 186-188 in your textbook (Hendricks) as examples. *Your outline does not need to be in chart form.*

2. The ***Theme*** of Philippians (What is it about?) - 15 words or less.

3. The ***Purpose*** of Philippians (Why was it written?) - 15 words or less.

* Don't forget to make two (2) copies of your homework

Review / Summary of Chapter 5
THE PRINCIPLE OF CONTEXT

I. Discover the Overall Context

    A. Discover the book **theme** – what the book is about.
    B. Discover the book **purpose** – its unique intent or reason for being written.

II. Discover the Immediate Context

    A. Understand the theme of the paragraphs before and after your text.
    B. State the theme of the paragraph you are developing
    C. Write down anything that's unclear or confusing.

Chapter 6
Principles of Grammar pt. 1

Paragraphs are the key unit of thought in written communication. Every paragraph consists of one or more sentences. A sentence is different words connected together to form a structured thought. Grammatical laws govern that structure. Like the standards for bricks, plywood, and studs in the building code, so grammatical laws bind sentences together. Grammar largely determines what the sentence means.

I. The Importance of the Principle of Grammar

Our era greatly downplays the concept of grammar. Indeed, you may be frightened or dismayed just by having read the last paragraph. However, if you are going to read the Bible well, you must discover and appreciate the grammatical relationships of words in the sentence. Jesus did.

In ***Matthew 22:23-33***, Jesus based his beliefs in resurrection on one ***grammatical*** point. It was the verb tenses in Exod. 3:6 repeated in Matt. 22:32. Jesus noted that God said, "**I Am** the God of Abraham, Isaac and Jacob." The verb "am" is the present tense of the verb "to be." God "**is**" – right now, the God of men who died physically centuries before Moses saw the burning bush. The verb tense determines the meaning.

In Luke 20:41-44, Jesus based His conclusion on the object of the sentence: "Lord." Jesus clearly demonstrates the importance of carefully reading the grammar of a passage. The principle of grammar teaches you that meaning is expressed according to the relationships of words in a sentence.

You will never make errors when you interpret the Bible the same way Jesus did. He observed grammar, such as the tense of a verb. So should we.

There are three key things to grasp about grammar. One is the **_structure_** of the sentence and/or paragraph. The second is the **_function_** of the words in the sentence. Last is the way the words and ideas **_connect_**.

II. Look for Sentence and Paragraph Structure

Every sentence and paragraph has structure. That is, it's built on a certain foundation and has a specific shape. Very often, sentence structure is one of six main types. **There are many more, but these six are the most common**. When you recognize them, you are well on your way to understanding the sentence.

    A. **_Explanation or reason_**: An idea is presented and then explained or supported. The idea usually appears in one sentence and the explanation follows in the next. Explanatory sentences contain the word "for" or "because" (Matt. 7:13-14; Mark 12:43-44; Rom. 5:9-10; Titus 3:1-3).

    From the above list of Scriptures, let's use Mt. 7:13, 14 as an example, *"Enter through the narrow gate;* **for** *the gate is wide and the way is broad that leads to destruction, and there are many who enter through it.* **For** *the gate is small and the way is narrow that leads to life, and there are few who find it."* Jesus commands His listeners to enter through the narrow gate. He then gives two explanatory reasons, both marked by the words "for".

    We do this sort of thing in everyday life all the time. "I am going to the store **_for_** some eggs and milk." I might tell my child to clean her room. When she asks why, I say, "Because I said so" or "Because we have company coming." These are explanatory sentences, and you will do well to begin to notice them when you study the Bible, (if you do not do so already).

B. **_Repetition_**: Terms or phrases are repeated for emphasis (Matt. 7:7-8; Phil. 4:4; Heb. 1:5; 1 Pet. 2:7-8).

Again, from the list above, let's use Matt. 7:7, 8 as an example:
"Ask, and it will be given to you; seek, and you will find; knock, and it will be opened to you. For everyone who asks receives, and he who seeks finds, and to him who knocks it will be opened." A person could be a new child of God, having never read his Bible before, and with a careful reading of the verse observe that, "ask", "seek," and "knock" are each used twice in these two verses. Whatever else these verses might teach, asking, seeking, and knocking are important.

We tend to communicate similarly. When something is very important to us, we say it over and over. When I was a boy, we had a screen door off the back of our house. In the spring and fall, when the weather was not too hot or cold, we would keep the other door open with only the screen door closed. When leaving the back door in a hurry, I would run out the screen door and the giant spring would close it with a bang. My dad would say, "Billy, how many times do I have to tell you not to slam the door?" Repetition is a great teacher.

C. **_Contrast_**: Two or more words or ideas that are unlike or dissimilar. These sentences often contain "but" and/or "yet" (Mt. 6:19-21, Eph. 2:1-4).

In Ephesians 1-3, Paul writes to remind the Ephesian saints of their wealth. To teach this great truth, he reminds them of their past poverty. *"And you were dead in your trespasses and sins, in which you formerly walked according to the course of this world, according to the prince of the power of the air, of the spirit that is now working in the sons of disobedience. Among them we too all formerly lived in the lusts of the flesh, indulging the desires of the flesh and of the mind, and were by nature children of wrath, even as the rest.* ***But*** *God, being rich in mercy, because of His great love with which He loved us...."* (Eph. 2:1-4, emphasis mine). Paul paints a rather grim picture of his, and their, past spiritual poverty. The entire passage changes on a little word, "but." It is a pivotal word that contrasts their past as spiritually bankrupt unbelievers from the present as spiritually rich saints.

D. **_Comparison_**: Two or more words or ideas that are alike or similar. Do you remember similes and metaphors from high school English class? Similes often contain "like" or "as" BUT metaphors do not. (Luke 3:22; John 3:8, 12, 14; 1 Pet. 2:1-3).

First Peter 2:2 says, "***Like*** *newborn babies, long for the pure milk of the word, so that by it you may grow in respect to salvation."* Peter does not say his readers, past or present, are babies. He only compares them for a specific reason. Just as babies need milk to grow physically, so too believers need the Word of God to grow spiritually.

E. **_Continuation_**: A progression of events or ideas that are usually connected by "and" or "or" or "likewise" or by the use of a comma. Philippians 4:12, *"I know how to get along with humble means, and I also know how to live in prosperity; in any and every circumstance I have learned the secret of being filled and going hungry, both of having abundance and suffering need."* Do you see several continuations? (See also Titus 2:6 and 1 Pet. 2:13-14, 3:1). Commas and the word "and" are the most common continuations.

F. ***Summarization* or application**: One event, idea, concept, or action is summarized or applied to the reader. These sentences often start with the word "therefore." As others before me have noted, "When you see a therefore, see what it's there for." When you spot that term, always look at what came before it to determine the summary or application (Matt. 28:18-20; Mark. 12:35-37).

Romans 12:1, *"**Therefore** I urge you, brethren, by the mercies of God, to present your bodies a living and holy sacrifice, acceptable to God, which is your spiritual service of worship."* God, through Paul's pen, commands believers to present the thing we value most in life, our bodies, to Him as a living sacrifice. On what basis should anyone obey this command? In part, the answer lies in the Paul's summary of the mercies of God which he has just spelled out for several chapters.

III. Notice the Functional Words in the Sentence

Every sentence contains functional words. These words help you recognize emphasis and grasp the overall concept. The following functional terms are the most significant. Learn to identify them in the sentences you study. Some basic functional parts and questions to ask when reading a passage are:

A. **Subject**: Ask, "Who is acting?" to locate the main ***subject***. The subject of a sentence does the acting or is acted upon. Sometimes the subject is implied rather than stated. Philippians 2:3 exhorts us, "***Let each of you regard one another as more important than himself***: "**Each of you**" is the subject.

B. **Verb**: Ask, "What does the subject do?" to discover the ***verb***. Verbs are the action words that tell you who does what. The verb indicates the action, state, or condition of or about the subject. It may place the action in the past, present, or future. Again, in Philippians 2:3, "***Let each of you regard one another as more important than himself***" "**regard**" is the verb. Additionally, it is important to note the tense of the verb. Is it past, present, or future? There is a world of difference! Suppose I told a student I *had given* (past tense) him a million dollars. He would have a large sum of money and many friends! However, if I said I *will give* (future tense) him a million dollars, he has nothing right now.

C. Object: When you ask "What or who receives the action?" you are looking for the ***object***. The object is who or what the subject **acts** upon. In Philippians 2:3 *"Let each of you regard one another as more important than himself"*, **"One another"** is the object.

D. Modifiers: Also ask "What do I learn about the main parts of the sentence?" Such ***modifiers*** enlarge the meaning of the words they modify. In Philippians 2:3, *"Let each of you regard one another as more important than himself"* **"As more important than himself"** is the modifier.

IV. Study the Connecting Words in the Sentence

How do the various terms and thoughts connect? Prepositions and conjunctions are words indicating connections and relationships. They are some of the most important words in the Bible. Train yourself to pick them out right away.

A. ***Prepositions*** are the little words that tell you where the action or relationships take place: in, on, upon, through, to, and so on. "***To*** *all the saints* ***in*** *Christ Jesus who are* ***in*** *Philippi*" (Phil. 1:1). When I was in junior-high school struggling to learn prepositional phrases, my teacher taught me something to help me remember what a preposition was. Instead of trying to memorize a long list of them, she said, "Billy, a preposition is anything a squirrel can do to a tree." I knew a few things about squirrels, they could go under, over, around, in, beneath, to (etc.) a tree. A preposition relates to direction, location or place, they relate one clause to another.

B. **_Conjunctions_** are words that **_connect_** one thought with another. The following chart displays the most common conjunctions. Conjunctions help form the structures discussed above.

CONJUNCTIONS			
Time Connectors	**Location Connectors**	**Logical Connectors**	**Emphatic Connecter**
After As Before Now Then Until When While	Where Wherever Whence	**Reason**: for, since **Results**: then, therefore, thus **Purpose**: so that, that **Contrast**: but, much more, nevertheless, otherwise, yet **Continuation**: and, even, also **Comparison**: as, just as, likewise, also **Condition**: if, if then	Indeed Only

V. Do a _diagrammatical layout_ of each sentence.

When you have located/observed the functional words in a sentence, the other words are essentially modifiers of the function words. Note the following examples of how this is to be done. The next page illustrates grammatical layout, or diagramming sentences, as it is sometimes referred to. A helpful resource you might want to obtain is *Diagramming the Scriptures* by Shirley M. Forsen (Xulon Press, 2010).

How does one go about diagramming a sentence or doing a grammatical layout? In addition to the book cited above, two helpful web pages to consider are:

- grammar.ccc.commnet.edu/grammar/ppt/diagrams.pps

- drb.lifestreamcenter.net/lessons/TS/diagram.htm

They are both excellent tutorials in the process (the first more in depth while the second is much more elementary).

For our purposes, let me offer a few suggestions for beginners. The basics are:
1. Diagramming sentences provides a way of <u>picturing</u> the structure of a sentence.
2. Place the <u>subject-verb</u> relationship on a straight horizontal line.
3. <u>Modifiers</u> go below the words they modify on slanted lines.
4. The <u>direct object</u> follows the verb on the horizontal line.
5. <u>Prepositional phrases</u> are arranged on branches below the words they modify.

See charts on the next page for basic illustrations of these principles.

Diagramming Sentences

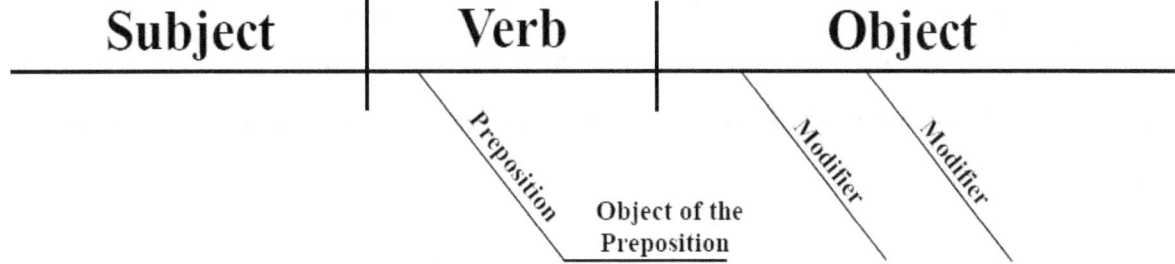

Fred drank some water inside his screened-in porch.

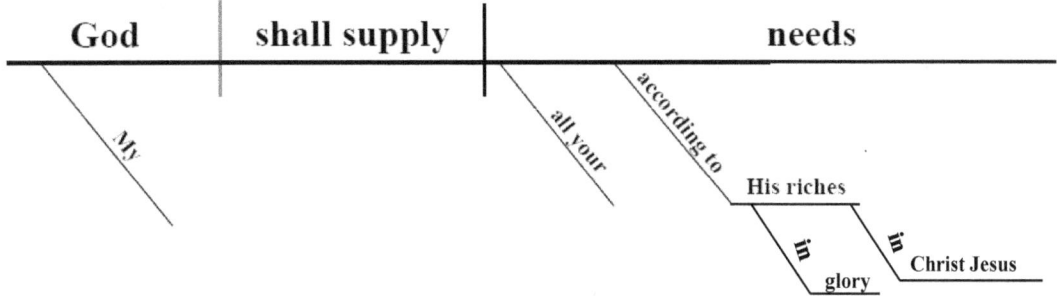

And my God shall supply all your needs according to His riches in glory in Christ Jesus.   Philippians 4:19

Diagramming sentences will enable you to better see the parts of a sentence, much the way the "pieces of the puzzle" fit together.

Most Bible students ignore or are intimidated by the principle of grammar. Not you though – you are better than that! Let this introduction to the importance of grammar motivate you. **Think of the great and awesome gems you will dig out of the mine of Scripture as you develop your grammatical abilities. It's really worth the effort**.

> **Now You Try It #6**
> Review this chapter including the following summary page. Read the next chapter in *Digging Deeper* and be prepared to discuss it. Write down any questions your reading generates. Read chapter 36-37 in *Living by the Book*. Finally, complete the assignment your teacher gives you and turn it in next class.

Homework Assignment #6* Two copies please.

Reading through Philippians find at least two explanations, two contrasts, two comparisons, two continuations, two repetitions, and two summarizations. Write them down along with the chapter and verse(s) they are located in. Come prepared to share with the class and turn in.

As an example of your homework:

1. Phil. 2:1 - Summarization. "Therefore"

Explanations:
   1.
   2.
Contrasts:
   1.
   2.
Continuations
   1.
   2.
Repetitions
   1.
   2.
Comparisons:
   1.
   2.
Summarizations:
   1.
   2.

Additionally, choose one verse/sentence from Philippians (but not 4:19) to diagram as illustrated and explained.

Review / Summary of Chapter 6
THE PRINCIPLE OF GRAMMAR

I. The Importance of the Principle of Grammar
    A. The principle of grammar teaches you that **meaning is expressed according to the relationships of words in a sentence**.
    B. There are three key things to grasp about grammar. One is the **structure** and/or paragraph. The second is the **function** of the words in the sentence. Last is the way the words and ideas **connect**.

II. Look for Sentence types
    A. **Explanation or Reason**: An idea is presented and then explained or supported.
    B. **Repetition**: Terms or phrases are repeated for emphasis.
    C. **Contrast**: Two or more words or ideas that are unlike or dissimilar.
    D. **Comparison**: Two or more words or ideas that are alike or similar.
    E. **Continuation**: A progression of events or ideas.
    F. **Summation or Application**: An event, idea, concept or action is summarized or applied to the reader.

III. Notice the Function Words in the Sentence
    A. Ask, "Who is acting?" to locate the main **subject**. The subject does the acting or is acted upon.
    B. Ask, "What does the subject do?" and you will discover the **verbs**, the action words that tell you who is doing what.
    C. When you ask, "What or who receives the action?" you are looking for the **object**. The object is who or what the subject **acts** upon.
    D. Also ask, "What do I learn about the main parts of the sentence?" Such **modifiers** enlarge the meaning of the words they modify.

IV. Study the Connecting Words in the Sentence
    A. Prepositions tell you **where** the action or relationships take place: in, on, upon, through, to, etc.
    B. Conjunctions **connect** one thought with another.

Chapter 7

Principles of Grammar pt. 2

Ever played a game when the rules were unclear to you? It's terribly frustrating to make a move, play a card, or take some other action only to find out later that it was not a wise move or action. How about when the rules are not even known, and someone is making them up as they go along? It's never fun to play such games. While Bible study is not a game, the student of Scripture would do well to understand that there are rules/principles that govern how to read/study the Bible. Both oral and written communication have rules that govern them. In spoken communication, things such as eye contact, volume, inflection, and timing are very important. If the speaker is monotone, never varying his speech patterns, the audience will soon "tune out." If the speaker whispers, she will not be heard by her intended audience.

Written communication has many rules too. A good writer will know and adhere to these rules. God the Holy Spirit wrote the Bible using people (2 Tim 3:16; 2 Pet. 1:21), and He knows and understands how humans communicate and since He desires those who read the Bible to understand it. He revealed God's message to us using rules of written communication.

These rules include, though they are not limited to, grammatical principles. Do you recall studying English grammar in middle school or high school? For some it was upon coming to the United States as adults and being thrust into a second or third language. Being familiar with English grammar will greatly enhance your ability to study the Bible. Most followers of Christ in the United States will never learn Hebrew and Greek sufficiently enough to study the Bible from the original languages; therefore, the study of the English Bible must suffice.

1. NOUNS

Merriam-Webster defines a noun as, "A noun is a word that refers to a thing (book), a person (Betty Crocker), an animal (cat), a place (Omaha), an idea (justice), or action (yodeling)."

Another definition of nouns would be they are people, places, things or qualities. As for nouns being things:

- The **stone** was large and round.
- The **house** was in the mountains.
- The **leaves** were vibrant.

As stating earlier, at times nouns are qualities such as:

- **Truth** was hard to come by.
- **Honesty** is the best policy.
- **Beauty** is in the eye of the beholder.

A COMMON noun might be a person, place, or thing that is NOT definite. (e.g., man, prophet, child or town).

- The **man** went fishing.
- The **girl** left her doll on the park bench.
- The **town** was deserted due to the hurricane.

A PROPER noun is specific and names the person (e.g., Paul, John, Mary) or place (e.g., Jerusalem, Jericho, Egypt, Tarsus). Proper nouns are capitalized while common nouns are not.

- **Sarah** laughed at the news.
- **David** slung the stone.
- **Jerusalem** is the capital of **Israel**.

A. NOUNS AS SUBJECT

In a sentence, there will always be a noun used as the subject. At times, though, the subject is implied in the sentence, not written. Some instances where the subject is implied would be:
- Get out of my house! (Implied subject is "Thief")
- Beware of false teachers! (Implied subject is "believers").

As examples, see the following verses. Can you identify the implied subjects?
- The next day He purposed to go into Galilee, and He found Philip. And Jesus said to him, "Follow Me." John 1:43
- "Abide in Me, and I in you. As the branch cannot bear fruit of itself unless it abides in the vine, so neither *can* you unless you abide in Me." John 15:4
- preach the word; be ready in season *and* out of season; reprove, rebuke, exhort, with great patience and instruction. 2 Tim 4:2

As always, context will control the meaning and give a clear indication on who the subject of the sentence is.

Often, however, the subject will be quite clear and stated explicitly.
- **Abraham** believed God and it was counted to him as righteousness.
- **Ruth** gleaned in the fields of Boaz.
- **Moses** threw his staff on the ground.

B. NOUNS AS GERUNDS

It may have been a while since you've heard the word "gerund." What is it? A gerund could well be described as a "verbal noun." That is, it's a word that is used as a noun but often includes action. Gerunds often end with the letters "ing," "ed," or "en."
- **Running** is good exercise.
- **Swimming** is easier on the joints than other exercises.
- **Understanding** giveth favor (Prov. 13:15).

C. NOUNS AS OBJECTS

Nouns can also be the object of the sentence. That is, they receive the "action" of the verb. Perhaps when you were in school in the past, your teacher referred to them as "direct objects".

- Mary baked a **cake**.
- Alan twisted his **ankle**.
- Jared dunked a **basketball**.
- "He reproved **kings** for their sakes" Psalm 105:14.
- "He leadeth **me** beside still waters" Psalm 23:2
- "He shall feed His **flock** like a shepherd" Isaiah 40:11

2. PRONOUNS

Pronouns are those words that take the place of nouns. It would get old and tiresome if a writer wrote of her friend Betsy and kept using the name Betsy with no variation. After introducing Betsy, the author, if she's a good one, will vary her story to include words like "she" and "her" when referring to Betsy. The "she" and "her" are the pronouns.

A. PERSONAL PRONOUNS

Personal pronouns are words that refer to specific people. They include, but are not limited to words like: I, me, my, you, us, we, etc.

What are the personal pronouns in the following two verses?

- Isaiah 45:22
- Matthew 6:25

B. INDEFINITE PRONOUNS

These to not refer to any definite person, place or thing. As examples, "Whoever," "many," "all," "anyone," and "everyone."

Can you locate the indefinite pronouns in the following verses?

- Romans 14:7
- Romans 14:23

C. Reflexive Pronouns

These end with "self" or "selves." Examples of reflexive pronouns would be "myself," "ourselves," "himself," "itself," and "themselves."

Can you locate the reflexive pronouns in the following verses?

- 1 Samuel 3:21
- Proverbs 16:4 (KJV)

D. Interrogative Pronouns

An interrogative is a word that asks a question. Therefore, an interrogative pronoun is a pronoun that introduces a question.

- **Who** broke the lock?
- **Whose** book is this?

Can you identify the interrogative pronoun in the following verse?

- See Esther 4:14c

3. VERBS

A verb is an "action" word. It has long been described as "an action or state of being".

- I **was** (state of being) sick last Friday.
- The deer **ran** through the field.
- Peter **cast** the net into the sea.

Verbs normally have "tense" associated with them (past, present or future). Present tense verbs often end with "ing". For example: "running" "playing" "hiding", "fasting", "praying", etc.

- Gideon **was hiding** in a winepress.
- The church gathered and **was praying** for Peter.
- Paul's **preaching** caused a riot.

VERB TESTER

Have you ever wondered what the verb is in a sentence? Here is a handy verb tester: Use the word I/You/He + <u>the word you think is the verb</u> = make sense? If it makes no sense, you've selected the wrong word as the verb.

4. ADJECTIVES

"Adjectives describe or modify – that is they limit or restrict the meaning of nouns and pronouns. They may name qualities of all kinds (*huge, red, angry, tremendous, unique, rare,* etc.)

Adjectives often fall into the following categories:

- <u>Color</u> <u>size</u> <u>kind</u>
- <u>Which?</u> <u>Whose?</u> <u>how many?</u>

- The **red** car crashed into the ditch.
- A **beautiful** bird flew past the window.
- The **fluffy white** snow covered the lawn.
- David chose **five smooth** stones.

Can you find adjectives in Genesis 30:37-40?

5. ADVERBS

An adverb is a part of speech used to describe a verb, adjective, clause or another adverb. It simply tells the readers how, where, when, or the degree to which something was done. Adverbs often end with "ly" as in: nicely, quickly, effortlessly, smoothly, completely, rudely, etc. - Elizabeth **quickly** finished cleaning her room.

- Dan **hurriedly** mowed his lawn.
- Jehu **furiously** drove his chariot.

Can you find adverbs in the following verses?

- 2 Cor. 12:15
- 1 Thes. 5:23

REVIEW:

1. A noun is a person, place, thing, or quality that may be used as either the subject of the sentence or the object of the sentence. At times the noun is understood, but not clearly stated in the sentence being studied.

2. Nouns might be either common nouns or proper nouns.

3. A gerund is a "verbal noun" that often includes some form of action.

4. Pronouns are the words that take the place of nouns. They might be personal (I, me, he, she, they), indefinite (all, whoever, anyone), reflexive (myself, ourselves, himself,) interrogative (Who? Whose?) or possessive (my, our, his, hers, ours).

5. Verbs are words that describe action or state of being (run, flee, was, is).

6. Verbs often reveal the tense of the action (past, present or future). Past tense verbs often end with "ed", though many have irregular endings (jumped, died, buried).

7. An adjective modifies or describes nouns or other adjectives. They limit the use of nouns or pronouns (red, big, old, sharp).

8. Adverbs often end with an "ly" and describe verbs, other adverbs or adjectives (quickly, slowly, repeatedly).

NOW YOU TRY #7

Read chapters 9, 10, 13, and 14 in *Living By the Book* and complete the following.

1. Find at least five (5) nouns in the book of Philippians. Note the chapter and verse for each.

2. Find at least five (5) proper nouns in the book of Philippians. Note the chapter and verse of each.

3. Find at least three (3) gerunds in the New Testament letters. Note the chapter and verse for each.

4. Find at least five (5) verbs/participles in Philippians. Note chapter, verse, AND tense (past, present or future).

5. Locate at least five (5) adjectives in Philippians. Note chapter and verse for each.

6. Find at least three (3) adverbs in Philippians. Note chapter and verse for each.

Chapter 8

THE PRINCIPLE OF WORD MEANING pt. 1

I. The Importance of Words

Words are the basic building blocks of a passage of Scripture. They form the sentences that create the paragraphs that are the basic unit of literary thought. We must understand how the authors used their words in their culture to grasp their full meaning. This principle is challenging because words have different meanings in different contexts and cultures, and because figures of speech, idioms, and word usage change over time.

To see how language changes, when I was a boy "bad" meant that you had been naughty. At least for now, "bad" means good (e.g., "That car is bad.") When my oldest daughter was a young girl, my wife and I would alternate nightly reading a chapter of a classic book to her before bedtime. I was reading the introduction to John Bunyan's *Pilgrim's Progress* and came across a word I did not know, "gael." I tried to sound it out phonetically and then realized, from the context, it was the word "jail." That is how much the English language has changed in four hundred years. In the King James' Version of the Bible, in Genesis 41:2-4 the word "kine" is used five times. I dare say that is not a word you have used in the last month or two. The newer translations use the word "cow." Four hundred years ago, "kine" was the normal word to use when speaking of a "cow." My, how times and language have changed!

The good Bible student remembers that the Old Testament is translated from Hebrew and the New Testament from Greek. She remembers, furthermore, that the English language itself has undergone changes since the King James Version of 1611. Therefore, the modern reader faces certain problems with words. Rarely does a word in one language mean precisely what the word of another language means. In studying the Scriptures, therefore, it is necessary to study crucial words in their original language to make sure you understand them properly in English. In part this chapter addresses the question, "Can a person do a quality word study without any knowledge of the Hebrew and Greek languages?" Does one have to go to Bible College or seminary to study the biblical languages for several years in order to truly grasp the meaning of God's Word? Can one really dig deep without such training? A brief answer is "yes!" One can be a very fine student of the Bible without an ability to read the Hebrew and/or Greek texts, though this inability will limit the student to some degree.

This principle teaches us **to understand the original meaning of the words in a sentence**. Jesus did this in Matthew 22:41-46. He challenged the Pharisee's lack of belief in Him on the basis of a particular word in Psalm 110 translated "Lord."

A. The Practice of Word Study

To do a word study the following approach is helpful. **See Word Study appendices** for example pages from various tools and steps to complete the process of a Word Study.

THE TRADITIONAL APPROACH TO WORD STUDY

Put another way, this is the "old fashioned," resources in hand, hard copy way of doing a word study.

> 1. Select the ***key word or words*** in the sentence that you wish to study. Put another way, you can't do a word study without a word to study! But how does one go about choosing a word? Suppose you are studying a passage with ten verses and a total of one hundred words. You couldn't possibly, nor would you need to, do a word study on all those words. So

which one(s) would you choose? You would want to choose the word(s) that you are sure you don't know their meaning(s). Additionally, you would want to choose a word that is the key word to the passage. For example, in Acts 16:31 the Philippian jailer asked Paul, "Sirs, what must I do to be saved?" You would definitely want to do a study on the word "saved" even though you might think you already know what it means.

2. Discover how your author uses that term.

    a. Look up the word in **_Strong's Concordance_** and note its number. In many concordances the italicized numbers are for New Testament words while regular numbers are for Old Testament words. The numbers are INDEXED in the back of the concordance. Write down what you find in the dictionary in the back of your Strong's. For example, the number in Strong's might be #6372. Write it down, even though at this point that number means nothing to you.

    Image from Strong's Concordance…

each one of you is to put aside and **save**, 1Co 16:2		2343
to **save** up for *their* parents,	2Co 12:14	2343
came into the world to **save** sinners,	1Tm 1:15	4982
the One able to **save** Him from death,	Heb 5:7	4982
He is able also to **save** forever those who	Heb 7:25	4982
which is able to **save** your souls,	Jas 1:21	4982
Can that faith **save** him?	Jas 2:14	4982
who is able to **save** and to destroy;	Jas 4:12	4982
way will **save** his soul from death and	Jas 5:20	4982
save others, snatching them out of	Jude 1:23	4982

Students often ask why they can't just use the concordance in the back of their Bible instead of purchasing an exhaustive concordance. The difference between the concordance in their Bible and an exhaustive concordance is similar to the difference between having a one-page map of the entire United States and an atlas of the fifty states. The detail in the latter is much greater; therefore, it is much more helpful (#3, #4, #5 and #6 on Word Study Check List). Be sure to write down the definition(s) of the word you are studying. You will find it in the appropriate dictionary in the back of Strong's (Greek or Hebrew).

Excerpt from Greek Dictionary section in Strong's Concordance…

4981 σχολή [*schole* /skhol·**ay**/] n f. Probably feminine of a presumed derivative of the alternate of 2192; GK 5391; AV translates as "school" once. **1** freedom from labour. **2** a place where there is leisure for anything, a school.

4982 ἐκσῴζω, σῴζω [*sozo* /**sode**·zo/] v. From a primary sos (contraction for obsolete saoz, "safe"); TDNT 7:965; TDNTA 1132; GK 1751 and 5392; 110 occurrences; AV translates as "save" 93 times, "make whole" nine times, "heal" three times, "be whole" twice, and translated miscellaneously three times. **1** to save, keep safe and sound, to rescue from danger or destruction. 1A one (from injury or peril). 1A1 to save a suffering one (from perishing), i.e. one suffering from disease, to make well, heal, restore to health. 1B1 to preserve one who is in danger of destruction, to save or rescue. 1B to save in the technical biblical sense. 1B1 negatively. 1B1A to deliver from the penalties of the Messianic judgment. 1B1B to save from the evils which obstruct the reception of the Messianic deliverance.

4983 σῶμα [*soma* /so·mah/] n n. From 4982; TDNT 7:1024; TDNTA 1140; GK 5393; 146 occurrences; AV translates as "body" 144 times, "bodily" once, and "slave" once. **1** the body both of men or animals. 1A a dead body or corpse. 1B the living body. 1B1 of animals. **2** the bodies of planets and of stars (heavenly bodies). **3** is used of a (large or small) number of men closely united into one society, or family as it were; a social, ethical, mystical body. 3A so in the NT of the church. **4** that which casts a shadow as distinguished from the shadow itself.

Whatever translation of the Bible you normally study from, purchase a concordance that is keyed to that translation (e.g., New International Version of the Bible, then you would want to purchase an NIV concordance).

b. Look for the same word ***elsewhere*** in the ***same*** book of the Bible you are studying. You will discover this by looking at the uses of the term in Strong's. Are any other usages of the same word (same Strong's #) listed in the same book of the Bible? Then, find all uses by the same author in the Bible. For example, if you were studying the word "save," you would note that the word is used five (5) times in James' epistle. Since James wrote no other books in the New Testament, you would not need to check its usage in other places. If you were studying "save" in I Peter, you would want to check to see if Peter used the word in his second letter. On some occasions the book of the Bible you are studying was written by a person who wrote only one book of the Bible, thus this step would be skipped (e.g., Matthew, James, Jude). Compare the translations to see how the author employs the word. Note the contexts carefully and summarize in writing what you discover.

C. There are many helpful resources available. Two of them you might want to use are *Vines Expository Dictionary,* if studying the New Testament, or *Theological Wordbook of the Old Testament* when studying an Old Testament word. To determine the word's root and contextual meanings. You might also consult with Richard's *Expository Dictionary of Bible Words* for a good summary of how the word is used throughout the Bible.

Excerpt from Vine's Dictionary...

SAVE, SAVING

A. Verbs.

1. *sozo* (σώζω, 4982), "to save," is used (as with the noun *soteria*, "salvation") (a) of material and temporal deliverance from danger, suffering, etc., e.g., Matt. 8:25; Mark 13:20; Luke 23:35; John 12:27; 1 Tim. 2:15; 2 Tim. 4:18 (KJV, "preserve"); Jude 5; from sickness, Matt. 9:22, "made ... whole" (RV, marg., "saved"); so Mark 5:34; Luke 8:48; Jas. 5:15; (b) of the spiritual and eternal salvation granted immediately by God to those who believe on the Lord Jesus Christ, e.g., Acts 2:47, RV "(those that) were being saved"; 16:31; Rom. 8:24, RV, "were we saved"; Eph. 2:5, 8; 1 Tim. 2:4; 2 Tim. 1:9; Titus 3:5; of human agency in this, Rom. 11:14; 1 Cor. 7:16; 9:22; (c) of the present experiences of God's power to deliver from the bondage of sin, e.g., Matt. 1:21; Rom. 5:10; 1 Cor. 15:2; Heb. 7:25; Jas. 1:21; 1 Pet. 3:21; of human agency in this, 1 Tim. 4:16; (d) of the future deliverance of believers at the second coming of Christ for His saints, being deliverance from the wrath of God to be executed upon the ungodly at the close of this age and from eternal doom, e.g., Rom. 5:9; (e) of the deliverance of the nation of Israel at the second advent of Christ, e.g., Rom. 11:26; (f) inclusively for all the blessings bestowed by God on men in Christ, e.g., Luke 19:10; John 10:9; 1 Cor. 10:33; 1 Tim. 1:15; (g) of those who endure to the end of the time of the Great Tribulation, Matt. 10:22; Mark 13:13; (h) of the individual believer, who, though losing his reward at the judgment seat of Christ hereafter, will not lose his salvation, 1 Cor. 3:15; 5:5; (i) of the deliverance of the nations at the Millennium, Rev. 21:24 (in some mss.). See SALVATION.

As you do word studies, you will soon discover that all words have what I will call a "range of meaning." Do you remember the word "trunk" from chapter 3? We discovered it could mean a box for sweaters, the bottom of a tree, a person's torso, the back end of a Chevy or an elephant's nose. This concept simply means the various ways the word is used in Scripture. For example, the word "save" is used to preserve from danger, to preserve a person from eternal punishment (hell), to heal a person from illness or disease, and to protect from physical harm (David saved from Saul). What is the range of meaning for the word you are studying? As you look at a word's various uses, you will discover the answer to this question.

D. Next, read the passage you are studying. Of the range of meaning, which of the meanings you discovered makes the most logical and contextual sense? What is the range of possible meanings for your word in this context? For example, the word "save" means "to protect, deliver; to make well; to heal." It was used often to protect someone from harm; to cure from illness; to protect from physical harm; and to deliver from sin, to save from hell. Which fits your passage best? That is probably the best use of the word in the passage you are studying. Read your passage again using your interpretation of the word. Does your interpretation fit the context? It is usually evident when it does not. Check your conclusion with a good commentary such as the *Bible Knowledge Commentary*. If need be, adjust your interpretation to fit what you have learned. Perhaps the commentary revealed something you had missed and gave you good reason to change your interpretation.

ELECTRONIC APPROACH TO WORD STUDY

You can do a word study using the internet as well. While there are several websites, the following method is based on BlueLetterBible.

Step 1: Go to www.blueletterbible.org.

Step 2: In the "Search the Bible" box at the top of the screen, enter James 1:21. If you are using a particular translation, then make that selection as well. For class, select NASB. Then click the green search icon in the lower right corner.

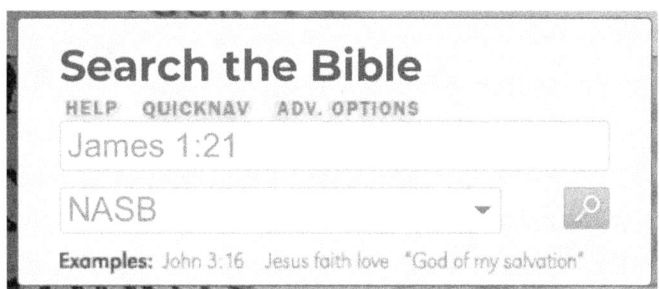

Step 3: In the list on the left, you'll see James 1:21. To the left of the verse, click on the "Tools" button.

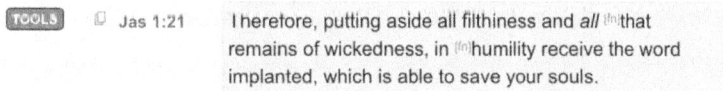

Step 4: After clicking on Tools, a pop-window will appear with a list of all the words. Scroll down until you find the word "to save." Click on the # under the Strong's column. For "save," the # is G4982.

*In the event you're searching an Old Testament word, the # will begin with "H" for Hebrew (G for Greek; H for Hebrew).

Step 5: The new window contains a host of information, including lexicon data, dictionary aids, translation count, and much more. From this window, you can now complete the word study process.

How to Complete the Word Study Checklist using BlueLetterBible

There are 10 steps in the Word Study Checklist (see Appendix). Here's how to complete each of those steps using BlueLetterBible.

1. **Choose a word** – Choose your word carefully as learned in class. Remember, you don't have time to do a word study on every single word in every verse every week.

2. **Look up the word in your concordance** – This step is completed using Steps 1–4 above.

3. **Write down the number** – The number you selected in Step 4 is the Strong's number. In the example of "save" in James 1:21, this number is G4982.

4. **Look up the number in the correct dictionary** – When you click the Strong's number (G4982), the new window that appears is a summary of the dictionary information. In this area, you can find the transliteration, part of speech, pronunciation, and much more. Be sure to write down the definition(s) of the word.

5. **Is the word (same #) used elsewhere in the same book (James)?** – To the right of the lexicon block, you should see an area for "Search Results By Book." Notice the abbreviated book name ("Jas" for James). The # in parentheses identifies the number of occurrences appears in this book. In this example, G4982 appears 5 times in James.

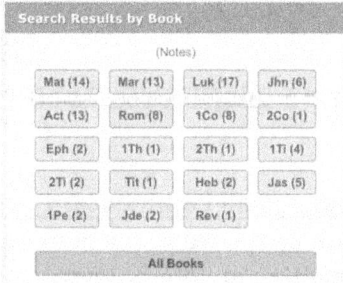

Click on "Jas (5)" to open a new window with these five occurrences listed.

6. **Is the word (same #) used elsewhere in a different book?** – In the case of James, there is no other book written by James. However, to complete this step, simply note the other results in the "Search Results by Book" area. Click on each book individually to read the verses in context.

7. **Look up your word in Vine's Expository Dictionary** – To complete this step, go back to the lexicon/dictionary screen. Scroll down to the "Dictionary Aids" section. Click on the "View Entry" link beside *Vine's Expository Dictionary*.

   > **Dictionary Aids**
   >
   > **Vine's Expository Dictionary:** View Entry
   > **TDNT Reference:** 7:965,1132

   *When studying a Hebrew word, you will notice TWOT (*Theological Wordbook of the Old Testament* by Harris, Archer, and Gleason) instead of *Vine's Expository Dictionary*. Unfortunately, BlueLetterBible does not connect you directly to the definition. Instead, you would need to look up the number listed in TWOT.

   > **Dictionary Aids**
   >
   > **TWOT Reference:** 2407a

   > **KJV Translation Count — Total: 110x**
   >
   > The KJV translates Strong's G4982 in the following manner: save (93x), make whole (9x), heal (3x), be whole (2x), *miscellaneous* (3x).

8. **What is the range of meaning for the word?** – To locate the other ways this Bible translation also translated G4982, scroll down to the Translation Count. In the case of G4982, the word is also translated "make," "whole," "heal," and "be whole."

   > **KJV Translation Count — Total: 110x**
   >
   > The KJV translates Strong's G4982 in the following manner: save (93x), make whole (9x), heal (3x), be whole (2x), *miscellaneous* (3x).

9. **What is your interpretation of the word in its context?** – This step is on you.

10. **What does a good commentary say about this word?** – This step requires you to look up the word in a commentary. Make sure to include the name of the commentary in your homework.

Review:

1. Word studies help the student of scripture dig more deeply into the meaning of words, going all the way to the original Greek or Hebrew.

2. There is a ten-step process that, when adhered to, will allow every student to successfully complete a word study.

3. Electronic word studies are a more efficient use of time and reduce the probability of "human error".

3. A word study process list is provided in appendices.

NOW YOU TRY # 8

Read chapters 16-20 in *Living By the Book.* Additionally…

Following the Word Study Process (see appendix) and the procedures mentioned in this chapter, complete one (1) word study from the book of Philippians. You would be wise to choose a word that will come from your final project passage (a passage you'd like to study to prepare to teach).

Complete all ten steps of the word study. Make a second copy to turn in at the beginning of the next class.

Chapter 9
THE PRINCIPLE OF WORD MEANING pt. 2

You've now completed a word study. For many, it was the first time you've ever done one. Perhaps it was challenging for you. Did you get confused? This lesson will build on the last and attempt to drive home more key truths about word studies.

Last lesson focused on how to do a word study. More specifically, how does a student of the English Bible dig deeply into the meaning of the original Hebrew or Greek word if she does not have the knowledge of either of the two languages? One response, and perhaps the best one, is to learn both languages in a Bible college or seminary. Short of that, are there other steps a person can take to complete a word study? In the last lesson we learned the answer was "yes!" You can take a few shortcuts to finding out the original meaning of words without a working knowledge of biblical languages.

Now that you've completed a word study, a first for most folks, you have a better idea of how the process works. As with many important skills, a bit of repetition might help you better understand and cement the process.

Importance of Word Studies

Hopefully the importance of doing word studies has become clear. If it has not, consider the following – In this course we've been studying the book of Philippians. In the King James Version of the Bible, we read in Philippians 3:15, "Let us, therefore, as many as be perfect…." At first glance many readers might see the word "perfect" and conclude, "Well, I'm not perfect!" Or, "That verse is only for those who have _everything_ together." A key word to study, then, would be "perfect." By the way, it doesn't mean what it appears to mean in the KJV.

Word studies not only help the student of Scripture understand the word's meaning, they also steer us clear of doctrinal heresy. A fairly new, yet growing, heresy is sometimes called "annihilationism." It teaches that God's central character trait is love. Therefore, He would never eternally punish people who reject Him. So instead He merely destroys them. To put it in modern vernacular, He "nukes" them into non-existence. This heresy believes it is supported biblically from Matthew 10:28, which says, "And fear not them which kill the body, but are not able to kill the soul: but rather fear him which is able to *destroy* both soul and body in hell" (KJV – italics mine).

At first glance, it may appear this belief has some biblical basis, that is until a word study is done (and the truth of the rest of scripture is brought to bear – see chapter 11 – Principle of Related Scripture).

When one does a word study on the word "destroy," he finds the word used of new leather patches sewn on old leather wineskins and the result is the skins are "destroyed." That is, they are "ruined, marred" (Luke 5:37). They become unfit for their intended purpose. The word has a range of meaning that can include: "to ruin, to mar, to perish, to destroy." The wineskins in Luke's account did not cease to exist, they merely could not hold wine due to their marred condition. Similarly, people who reject God will be unable to fulfill their intended purpose, namely praise and glorify their Creator.

RANGE OF MEANING

One step we discussed last week in our word study process was step eight (8), which we entitled, "range of meaning." Another phrase for that concept is "semantic range". Maybe that's a new concept for you. Maybe you have heard the phrase "it's just a matter of semantics." The idea is that words have different meanings in different contexts. If I think the word means one thing and you think the word means something very different, we will have some very fundamental differences when it comes to interpretation.

As discussed in the previous chapter, the word "save" is often thought to mean "go to heaven" or to "rescue from hell." While that is true at times, it is not the only meaning of the word. "Save" has a much broader range of meaning. As examples look at the following six (6) ways the term "save" can be used in the New Testament:

1. <u>Temporal</u> (in time, temporary) <u>deliverance from danger, suffering</u> – Matt. 8:25; Mark 13:20; Luke 23:35.

2. <u>Deliverance from sickness</u> – Matthew 9:22; Mark 5:34; Luke 8:48

3. <u>Eternal deliverance from the penalty of sin</u> – Acts 16:31; Eph. 2:5, 8; Titus 3:5 (Justification).

4. <u>Deliverance from the bondage of sin</u> – Matt. 1:21; Rom. 5:10; 1 Cor. 15:2; James 1:21 (Sanctification).

5. <u>Future deliverance from the presence of sin</u> – Rom. 5:9; 11:26 (glorification).

6. <u>Deliverance from The Tribulation into the kingdom</u> – Matt. 10:22; Mark 13:13 (tribulation saints).

There are *at least* six (6) ways the term "save" is used in the New Testament with a rather significant range of meaning. It can mean to deliver from danger, to deliver from illness, to deliver from hell, to deliver from the grip of sin, to deliver from the presence of sin and to deliver from the horrific trials and suffering of the tribulation to come. While the concept of deliverance runs through the entire range of meaning, the object of deliverance can be quite varied.

Can you see how wide the range of meaning, the semantic range, is for the word? Word studies will help you observe this concept. Ultimately, as the interpreter of Scripture, you will be required to determine which interpretation best fits the context of the passage you are studying.

DISCOVERING RANGE OF MEANING

How does a student of the Bible discover range of meaning? Remember when you did your last word study, we wrote down the Strong's number of the word?

Since we completed a word from the New Testament book of Philippians, it would have been a Greek word. If you completed your word study electronically, blueletterbible.com would have listed it as "G2389" with the "G" referring to "Greek." Using the Strong's number, you can look at where that word is listed in Strong's and discover the other places it is used in the New Testament.

1. Use Your Strong's Concordance.

For now, we will only consider how the author of the book you are studying used the word in the book we are studying (Philippians) and other books he wrote (all the books from Romans through Philemon). We will not consider the usage in other book of the New Testament by other authors. Additionally, we will not consider any Old Testament passages – since this is a word study, Old Testament passages are in Hebrew and therefore would not be the same word.

When you look at the word and the same Strong's number, you should discover if there are any other usages by same author in the same book of the New Testament AND same word by same author in other New Testament books (if applicable).

2. Consult a Dictionary/Lexicon.

As an example, Vine's is a helpful resource. Look up your word in English (e.g., "save"). What does it state about your word concerning range of meaning (semantic range)? It will list the ways the word is used from most common to least common, not most important to least important. Look up the verses listed and discover the context for each passage. If they fit the range of meaning suggested by the author, consider it as a part of the semantic range.

3. Summarize your discovery of the range of meaning.

After you are done the previous two steps, summarize all you've learned about the possible meanings of the word. Do you remember, from chapter 3, the word "trunk?" Its range of meaning included, "the nose of an elephant; the rear end of a car; the base of a tree; a container for storage in the attic; and a person's torso". That is a summary of the range of meaning for a word. When you've completed all these steps, you will be well on your way to discovering the word's meaning in the portion of Scripture you are studying.

REVIEW:

1. Word Studies are an important part of good hermeneutics. They guide us to discovery of the meaning of a passage of Scripture and guard us from heresy.

2. Range of meaning is the discovery of all the possible meanings of a specific Greek or Hebrew word as used in the Bible.

3. Range of meaning can be discovered by:

   A. Consulting Strong's exhaustive concordance.

   B. Considering Vine's Expository Dictionary (New Testament Greek words) or Theological Wordbook of the Old Testament (TWOT) by Harris, Archer, and Waltke (Old Testament Hebrew words).

   C. Summarize what you discovered about all the possible meanings of the word (also known as… the semantic range).

NOW YOU TRY #9

Read chapters 24-26 in *Living by the Book.* Additionally…

1. Complete an additional word study using any word in the book of Philippians. Be sure to include all ten steps from the Word Study Process appendix.

2. Additionally, complete a word study using a word from EITHER Psalm 23 OR Psalm 90 (this will be your first word study using Hebrew rather than Greek).

Chapter 10
LITERALLY?
Understanding Figurative Language

To declare "I must cram this book into my head" does not mean that I must literally cut open my cranium and stuff the book into my head. It means that I sense a strong need to gain an understanding of the concepts taught in the book. The language employed to communicate the idea is called a "figure of speech." We all use figurative language frequently as did the Lord. Remember when He called Herod a "fox" or proclaimed Himself the "Bread of Life"?

Of a sure business deal, we might say, "it's a slam dunk." Of a terrific sermon we might say, "he hit a home run".

WHAT ARE SOME COMMON FIGURES OF SPEECH YOU USE OR HEAR? Jot down several that come to mind…

-
-
-

1. APPRECIATING FIGURES OF SPEECH

A. Figures of speech use words and concepts with meaning other than their ordinary, natural sense. **All _cultures_ employ such language**. They give beauty and fragrance to speech. For instance, the use of a metaphor in "*The Lord is my Shepherd*" is a more picturesque way for David to express God's loving care for him than saying, "The Lord directs my life." Figurative language gives **mental pictures** to intended meanings. The images of figurative language are borrowed from daily life to illustrate a spiritual truth by giving impressive and/or memorable but still accurate descriptions.

B. Figures of speech do not violate the principle of plain meaning because every figure of speech communicates a plain, literal truth in its context.

C. **Figures of speech** usually communicate by **comparison**, contrast, substitution and / or exaggeration.

2. UNDERSTANDING FIGURES OF SPEECH

To interpret figures of speech is a simple two-part process.

A. Determine if a figure of speech is in the text. The following guidelines are suggested in Hendricks and Hendricks' book, *Living By the Book*, chapter 36, Figuring Out the Figurative.

- **Use the literal sense unless there is some good reason to not to**. (e.g., Song of Solomon – is not about Jesus' love for His bride, the church).

- **Use the figurative sense when the passage clearly tells you to do so**. (e.g., Pharaoh's dreams of corn and cows – Genesis 37).

- **Use the figurative sense if the literal sense is impossible or absurd**. (e.g., Rev 1:16 – sword out of Jesus' mouth).

- **Use the figurative sense if the literal sense would involve something immoral**. (e.g., John 6:53-55 – eating the body and blood of Jesus).

- **Use the figurative sense if a literal interpretation goes contrary to the context and scope of the passage**. (e.g., Rev 5:1-5 – Lion of the tribe of Judah; Ps 63:7 – In the shadow of Thy wings).

B. Discern the point of the figure of speech.

1. Select the *__image__* and *__referent__*. The image is the word picture or non-normal element. The referent is what the image refers to. For example, in "He flew down the road in his Porsche" the image is "a flying Porsche" and the referent is "he."

2. Is the point of comparison, contrast, etc. explained in the verse or immediate context?

3. If the point is not explained or immediately clear, consider the subjects being compared, contrasted, etc. Always apply the culture guideline. You must learn the qualities that the author knew the figure to have in his culture. If there are several cultural possibilities, sort them. When John wrote about the "Lamb of God", he might have had in mind the quality of humility, or the proneness to stray, or the responsibility of leadership, or of the substitute offering for sin. You would decide that the latter quality is the one John had in mind because it's in the text and fits the context. Be alert to the guideline of culture.

4. Write down the meaning and then check it. Does it fit the context? If so, press on. If not, reconsider your interpretation and adjust as demanded by the context.

C. KINDS OF FIGURATIVE LANGUAGE

The following is merely a brief, incomplete, list of the types of figurative language used in the Scriptures.

    1. **Anthropomorphism:** The attribution of human features to God. "Behold, the LORD'S hand is not so short that it cannot save; Nor is His ear so dull that it cannot hear" Isaiah 59:1.

    2. **Apostrophe:** Addressing a thing as if it were a person, or an object or imaginary person as if he were present. 1 Cor 15:55, "O DEATH, WHERE IS YOUR VICTORY? O DEATH, WHERE IS YOUR STING?"

3. **Hyperbole:** An understood exaggeration to make a clear point. "I robbed other churches by taking wages *from them* to serve you;" 2 Cor 11:8. Remember when Jesus said to pluck your eye out or to cut your hand off (Mt. 18:8, 9)? Those are both hyperboles.

4. **Litotes:** An ironic understatement in which an affirmative is expressed by the negative of its contrary (e.g., *you won't be sorry*, meaning *you'll be glad*). Other instances of a litotes would be, "*he's no dummy*" meaning "*he's smart*"; "it's not rocket science" meaning "*it's easy*".

Can you find a litotes in the following scriptures? Acts 19:23; 21:39 and Rev 3:5. What are they?

BELOW ARE SOME FIGURES OF SPEECH. LOOK AT THE EXAMPLES AND PRACTICE ON THOSE LEFT BLANK

FIGURE	IMAGE	REFERENT	MEANING
Jude 12	Clouds w/out water	They (apostates)	Apostates look and sound promising but are empty and profitless
Luke 13:32	That fox	Herod	The king is crafty and cunning
Mt. 7:7			
John 15:5			

1 Cor. 12:12			

Review 10
LITERALLY? Understanding Figurative Language

1. A figure of speech utilizes non-literal imagery to convey literal truths.

2. Figures of speech often compare, contrast, substitute or exaggerate.

3. When determining the meaning of the figure of speech, look of the image and referent.

4. Context and culture will direct the interpretation of the figure of speech.

5. Non-literal devices in the scriptures include similes and metaphors as well as:

- <u>anthropomorphism</u>, assigning human features to God.
- <u>apostrophe</u>, addressing a thing as if it were a person.
- <u>hyperbole</u>, an obvious exaggeration to make a point.
- <u>litotes,</u> an ironic understatement which affirms the opposite of what is stated.

> **NOW YOU TRY # 10**
>
> Read chapters 29, 30, and 32 in *Living by the Book*. Also…
>
> 1. Using the book of Philippians find two figures of speech. Be sure to note the image, referent AND your interpretation of the figure.
>
> 2. Using the book of Ephesians, find two more figures of speech. Be sure to note the image, referent AND your interpretation of the figure.

FINAL PROJECT REMINDER

Chapter 11

The Principle of Related Scripture

I. The Principle Summarized

An important means of assuring correct interpretation of a passage is to consult related passages within the Scriptures. The Bible itself is the best commentary on the Bible. This is often referred to as the "***analogy of faith***" principle in hermeneutics. Christ employs this principle in Mt. 22:34-40 when He ties together Dt. 6:5 and Lev. 19:18 to summarize the Old Testament. He also clarified the nature of divorce by using the analogy of faith in Mt. 19:3-9. Simply put, this principle teaches us to interpret Scripture by Scripture. McQuilken states the benefits of comparing Scripture with Scripture:

> The student should compare Scripture with Scripture, allowing the Bible to illumine itself. He should search for passages dealing with the same event or giving the same teaching, for passages with similar teaching and for passages with contrasting teaching. This gives insight into the meaning of the passage under study and ensures his interpretation is in harmony with the rest of scripture.[1]

II. The Necessity of Comparing Scripture with Scripture

The Bible forms a unit. It does not contradict itself; it complements itself. The New Testament is a commentary upon the Old Testament. The two testaments are two parts of the same book, not two separate books. The New Testament

---
[1] J. Robertson McQuilkin, *Understanding and Applying the Bible*, 182

epistles amplify the seed doctrines of the Gospels and Acts. Parallel passages are found in two or more of the Gospels: Samuel and Kings are parallel to Chronicles; portions of Ephesians and Colossians relate to each other, and portions of Romans and Galatians are similar. All sixty-six books of the Bible form essential parts of God's ***progressive revelation***. Though His disclosure of Himself to man is progressive, God's character is the same in every age, and His requirements and expectations for man's life may be added to or changed according to His will. It is wise, therefore, to consult verses in different parts of the Bible that discuss the same thing. Almost every doctrinal passage in Scripture has a parallel somewhere else in Scripture.

Not only, should a passage be compared with other passages that have similar teaching, it also should be compared with other passages that have contrasting teaching. You cannot fully understand the message of the Bible on a particular subject until you have considered all that the Bible says on the subject. Before you draw firm conclusions regarding a teaching that is merely implied in a Scripture passage, compare it with related passages. If the related passages support the implied teaching, then it may be considered biblical.

The following are some suggested ways to study the scriptures in unity, as a whole to insure we do not misinterpret it.

A. Compare Parallel passages by the same author.

Paul wrote at least thirteen letters/epistles of the New Testament. Some of them were written at nearly the same time chronologically, (the prison letters – Ephesians, Philippians, Colossians, and Philemon). The student of the Bible will want to consult the parallel truths in passages like these. For example, what truths do you gather from the following:

Ephesians 5:18-21   *compare with*   Colossians 3:15, 16
Ephesians 6:5-9   *compare with*   Colossians 3:22-4:1

B. Compare parallel passages by different authors.

The most obvious place to do this would be the four gospels. Some have called it a harmony of the gospels, when the student of scripture attempts to study parallel truths taught on two or more of the gospels. A most helpful resource is, *A Harmony of the Gospels* by Robert Thomas and Stanley Gundry. An example from another source is pictured below.

Jesus Before Pilate

(Matthew 27:2, 11-14; Mark 15:1-5; Luke 23:1-5; John 18:28-38)

Matthew	Mark	Luke	John
² And they bound him and led him away and delivered him over to Pilate the governor. ¹¹ Now Jesus stood before the governor, and the governor asked him, "Are you the King of the Jews?" Jesus said, "You have said so." ¹² But when he was accused by the chief priests and elders, he gave no answer. ¹³ Then Pilate said to him, "Do you not hear how many things they testify against you?" ¹⁴ But he gave him no answer, not even to a single charge, so that the	15 ¹ And as soon as it was morning, the chief priests held a consultation with the elders and scribes and the whole council. And they bound Jesus and led him away and delivered him over to Pilate. ² And Pilate asked him, "Are you the King of the Jews?" And he answered him, "You have said so." ³ And the chief priests accused him of many things. ⁴ And Pilate again asked him, "Have you no answer to make? See how many charges they bring against you." ⁵	23 ¹ Then the whole company of them arose and brought him before Pilate. ² And they began to accuse him, saying, "We found this man misleading our nation and forbidding us to give tribute to Caesar, and saying that he himself is Christ, a king." ³ And Pilate asked him, "Are you the King of the Jews?" And he answered him, "You have said so." ⁴ Then Pilate said to the chief priests and the crowds, "I find no guilt in this man." ⁵ But they were urgent, saying, "He stirs up	²⁸ Then they led Jesus from the house of Caiaphas to the governor's headquarters. It was early morning. They themselves did not enter the governor's headquarters, so that they would not be defiled, but could eat the Passover. ²⁹ So Pilate went outside to them and said, "What accusation do you bring against this man?" ³⁰ They answered him, "If this man were not doing evil, we would not have delivered him over to you." ³¹ Pilate said to them, "Take him

In the Old Testament, the books of 1 & 2 Samuel, 1 & 2 Kings and 1 & 2 Chronicles share many stories which should be considered by the diligent student of scripture.

For example, consider the following:

2 Samuel 24:1-10   *compare with*   1 Chronicles 21:1-8

C. Compare passages which contains similar ideas.

Like the previous two points, the concept here is to consult other places in the Bible that teach about the same concept. For example, the theme of the "great commission" should be considered from John 20:21, Matthew 28:19, 20, Luke 24:46-48 and finally, from Acts 1:8.

This same principle could be practiced on any topic of scripture. What does the Bible say about angels? What about giving? What about the use of spiritual gifts? The list of available topics is endless.

A commitment to this principle will be richly rewarding to the person who is disciplined enough to follow through, but it will not be without significant cost…time.

D. Compare scripture that contains contrasting ideas.

Remember, we're interested in discovering God's truth. Sometimes the truths of scripture ***appear*** to be in conflict but when studied can be clarified and melded together. For example, one person might describe a quarter as being so big, having a "bumpy" edge and having a likeness of George Washington on it. Another person might describe a quarter as being so big, having a "bumpy" edge and having a likeness of an eagle on it. Are those descriptions in conflict? Is either one a contradiction of the other? NO, they merely present truths that differ but can be reconciled, they are two sides of the same coin.

For example, some passages of scripture teach the humanity of Jesus (see Luke 2:7, 21, 52). Yet other passages of scripture teach the deity of Jesus (John 1:1, 2; 5:18; 39; Colossians 1:15-17). Many heresies have arisen in the past 2000 years since many people only believed one part of those two truths and failed to balance or complete them with the other.

On a less important level doctrinally, scripture teaches the believer to give generously (2 Corinthians 8 & 9) while at the same time teaching the believer to have a savings account, a "rainy-day" fund (Proverbs 6:6-8). We're commanded to not judge (Matthew 7:1; Romans 14:4) yet commanded to judge ("test the spirits" – 1 John 4:1, 6). Proverbs 26:4 says to not answer a fool according to his folly, while the next verse, 26:5 says to answer the fool lest he think himself wise. The point here is NOT for us to study and come to agreement in this lesson, but to understand the concept and the importance of the principle of correlating scripture with scripture.

E. Let the Old Testament Clarify the New Testament

There are sections of the New Testament that cannot be understood correctly apart from the Old Testament. The authors of the gospels, Acts, epistles and Revelation were schooled in the Old Testament. It colored their writings throughout the New Testament. Be as aware as possible of how the New Testament authors employed the Old in their writings. Notice the following examples. Read and check them.

1. John 1:51 and Genesis 28:10-12

2. John 20:12 and Exodus 25:10-22

3. Ephesians 3:17-21 and Exodus 40:1-38

F. Let the New Testament Clarify the Old Testament

1. This principle is seen when studying 2 Peter 2:2-4 and comparing it with Jude 6 and Genesis 6:1-13. When I was in Bible College, each student took a required class which was an in-depth exposition of Genesis. As part of the class, each student had to write a research paper on Genesis 6:1-4. It is a passage that has generated much discussion over the years. No matter what one's interpretation of the passage, much clarity is brought to it by the two other passages in Jude and 2 Peter.

2. Acts 4:23-31 and Psalms 2:1-2

G. Allow the New Testament to explain the New Testament

1. 1 Timothy 5:17-18 and Luke 10:7, Matthew 10:10 and Deuteronomy 25:4

2. James 5:14 (sick) and Hebrews 12:3 (weary) are both the same Greek term.

III. The Process of Scripture Interpreting Scripture

Use the cross-references in a Study Bible or your Concordance to locate passages related to the passage under study. A cross-reference book such as **Treasury of Scripture Knowledge** lists even more cross-references. Make sure you keep all cross-references in context and be sure that all the words are being used in the same way. If the topic you are studying is doctrinal, a theology book on the subject will offer additional help in locating both similar and contrasting passages. When you compare cross-references, be sure to pay close attention to the context.

Observe the texts carefully to see what they reveal about the subject you are studying. Make careful notes and be thoughtful as you think through your insights. Observe all the principles of hermeneutics we have previously studied. After comparing and contrasting, summarize your conclusions in a few brief words. Try for a sentence or two. Conclude by checking yourself with good commentaries.

Comparing Scripture with Scripture is a key element to reading the Bible well. The Bible is truth (John 17:17) but **no one passage contains all the truth**. If your interpretation of a passage violates what God has clearly said in another place, your interpretation must be changed/adjusted. As an
example, if I interpreted a passage to say that Jesus was merely human and not divine, I would be violating what God's Word clearly teaches. Is Jesus' human? Yes, but He is eternal (Isaiah 9:6, 7), the Word (John 1:1, 2), the creator (John 1:3; Col. 1:16). If I maintain that Jesus is human, I am correct, but to maintain that He was only human, is a serious heresy and violates the teaching of the Bible and the principle of related scripture. It would be similar to saying that the complete description of my father is that he is my father. True he is my dad, but he is also an uncle, a husband, a brother, a grandfather, a brother-in-law, friend and much more.

> **Now You Try It # 11**
>
> Review this chapter including the following summary page. Write down any questions your reading generates. Read chapters 21 – 23 in *Living by the Book*. Finally, complete the assignment your teacher gives you and turn it in next class.

Homework Assignment #11:

Answer the following questions from the appropriate chapter in *Living by the Book*. Write down your answer and come prepared to discuss in class.

1. In Chapter 21, what does "things related" refer to?

2. What are some things alike in Chapter 22?

3. What does Hendricks mean by "true to life" in Chapter 23?

4. In Acts 16, Luke records Paul's first visit to Philippi. What does the passage let you know about the founding of the church in that city? <u>Write a brief summary of what occurred during that visit.</u>

* REMEMBER: Two copies of your homework

Review / Summary of Chapter 11
THE PRINCIPLE OF RELATED SCRIPTURE

I. The Principle Summarized

The Bible is the best commentary on itself, so let Scripture interpret Scripture.

II. The Necessity of Comparing Scripture with Scripture
- A. The Bible forms a complementary unit, so compare similar passages.
- B. The Bible was revealed progressively, so compare contrasting texts.

III. The Process of Scripture Interpreting Scripture
- A. Compare parallel passages by the same author.
- B. Compare parallel passages by different authors.
- C. Compare passages which contain similar texts.
- D. Consider passages which contain contrasting ideas.
- E. Let the New Testament clarify the Old Testament.
- F. Let the Old Testament clarify the New Testament.
- G. Allow the New Testament to explain the New Testament.

The Practice Of Reading the Bible Well

Applying the Skills to Understand the Bible

Chapter 12
Observing the Text

There are few things in life as exciting and memorable as discovery. Knowing that you found a rare gem or recovered a long-lost family heirloom bring great satisfaction. You feel good about yourself, the world looks brighter and you are motivated. That's part of the privilege of Bible study too. Except here you discover truths about God, Christ, people and yourself, that not only encourage and motivate, they transform!

The repeated application of three simple skills make your hermeneutics live. These skills, although simple, require ***time*** and ***practice***, though they are separate skills, they are vitally related to one another. That is why you need to develop each one. You'll discover that the more adept you become at using them, the more the truths of Scripture will become obvious to you. You'll be awed at the wealth of spiritual riches contained in even the shortest passages – and you will have discovered them yourself! These three basic skills are ***observation***, ***interpretation*** and ***application***.

Let's get acquainted with observation in this chapter. Observation answers this question: ***What does the passage say***? The best Bible students are the best observers.

I. Observation Begins with Reading

Reading is the first technique you need to apply to get the most out of the passage. It is the foundational skill on which accurate understanding and application will grow. Learn to read your Bible with your eyes, your mind and your emotions along with a little imagination. When reading the Bible, do the following. Remember that our basic unit of study is the paragraph and that each paragraph is in the context of its book.

- Have a well-lit area, quiet location with a **_translation_** you understand.
- Read **_aloud_** whenever possible. This gives you a triple exposure to the Word – eyes, ears and speech.
- Read with **_feeling_**. Emphasizes the attitudes and emotions in the text.
- Read at **_conversational_** speed, as if you were talking to the author.
- Read to **_get the point_**. What's the primary message?
- Read for the **_big picture_**. See how the book fits together. Do the entire book at one sitting if possible.
- Read **_repeatedly_**. Go through the paragraph at least five times.

II. Observation Progresses with Seeing

The second skill to develop is to look **_carefully_** at the text and see what's there. You won't find every type of sentence in every passage, but these questions are the shovels that move the dirt, the dynamite that shatters the rock, the crane that lifts the load. Keep digging until you discover the message of the text. There are five key things to look for as you read and observe the paragraph, chapter or book.

   A. Look for things that are **_emphasized_** Biblical authors emphasize ideas in **_at least_** 3 ways.

   1. They may state their main point plainly (John 20:30; 1 Timothy 3:15–16). Parents do this too, when they kneel down and say to a child, "This is very important, daddy/mommy wants you to…."

   2. The amount of space they give to a topic, idea or event (see 2 Timothy 3:10-4:2 and the space devoted to "Scripture"). Again, we do the same thing, if it is important, we talk or write about it in great length.

3. The order of people, locations, events and ideas can call attention to something (Acts 1:8; Mark 3:13-19). In the Acts passage, the geography mentioned in order is: Jerusalem, Judea & Samaria and the uttermost parts of the earth. That is where the events of Acts unfold; Jerusalem (chapters 1-7); Judea & Samaria (chapters 8-12) and the uttermost parts (chapters 13-28, the missionary journeys).

B. Look for things that are ***repeated***, repetition is a key teaching tool.

1. Words, phrases, ideas or events (Ps. 136; Mk 11:32, 12:12; Heb. 11; 1 Cr. 15:12-28). Psalm 136 has 26 verses and 26 times the author declares the fact that God's mercy endures forever! In Hebrews 11 the word faith occurs many times and the phrase, "by faith" occurs 15 times. Perhaps the author is trying to make a point?!

2. People and/or names (Nicodemus through John; Mk. 12:28, 35, 38). In Matthew 23 Jesus said, "Woe to you scribes, Pharisees and hypocrites…" seven times!

C. Look for things that are ***alike***.

1. Carefully note the words "like" and "as." These signal a comparison. In John 3:14 Jesus compares Himself to the bronze serpent in the wilderness (Numbers 21:9). Clearly Jesus is not the same as the serpent, only similar in some fashion, ask yourself, what is the point of comparison?

2. Watch for comparisons ***without*** "like" and "as" (John 1:36, 15:1). In these cases, the comparison is merely implied, not stated. When the comparison is not stated it is called a metaphor.

D. Look for things that are ***different/unlike***. These are usually marked out with the word, "but" which indicates contrast (Eph. 2:4, 13).

E. Look for things that are ***true to life***. That is, what things in the text are like our life experiences? The people in Scripture didn't wear halos and white robes with belts of gold lace. They were power hungry, manipulative, agenda driven, ambitious, depressed, deceitful, honest, tired, happy, alone, leaders and followers just as we are. Let the true-life elements of the text flow through your reading. This helps bring it to life although we are several thousand years removed.

A word of caution/clarification is in order. Please note that I am NOT saying look for things that are true. The Bible is all truth (John 17:17). I am advocating for looking for *true to life* things. True to life would be something like paying taxes, which were required in first century Israel just as for us in twenty-first century America. The part that is NOT true to life is that we don't pay ours with a denarius.

III. Observation Benefits with Writing

Whenever you observe, write down what you discover. Construct some way to keep a record of what you see. You won't have memory lapses if you write them down. You will be able to compare your progress later. You will learn it better because you in-take through the eye and the hand. Finally, it aids you in the next step, interpretation. As the first skill needed, observation is foundational to the successful uses of the others. So, learn to read, see and write!

> **Now You Try It # 12**
>
> Review this chapter including the following summary page. Write down any questions your reading generates. Read chapters 27 – 28 in *Living by the Book*. Finally, complete the assignment your teacher gives you and turn it in next class.

Homework Assignment #12:

Read through Philippians and write down ten observations: 2 things emphasized, 2 repeated, 2 alike, 2 unlike and 2 true to life. Make sure to jot down chapter and verse. Come prepared to share with the class next week.

As an Example:
   1. Repetition: "Rejoice" in Phil 4:4

Emphasized:
  1.
  2.

Repeated:
  1.
  2.

Alike:
  1.
  2.

Unlike:
  1.
  2.

True to life:
  1.
  2.

* Two copies please.

Review / Summary of Chapter 12
OBSERVING THE TEXT

I. Observation Begins with Reading

- Have a well-lit, quiet location with a **translation** you understand.
- Read **aloud** whenever possible. This gives you a triple exposure to the Word – eyes, ears and speech.
- Read with **feeling**. Emphasizes the attitudes and emotions in the text.
- Read at **conversational** speed, as if you were talking to the author.
- Read to **get the point**. What's the primary message?
- Read for the **big picture**. See how the book fits together. Do the entire book at one sitting if possible.
- Read **repeatedly**. Go through the paragraph at least five times.

II. Observation Progresses with Seeing

    A. Look for things that are emphasized.
    B. Look for things that are repeated.
    C. Look for things that are alike.
    D. Look for things that are different/unlike.
    E. Look for things that are true to life.

III. Observation Benefits with Writing

Write down what you discover.

Chapter 13
INTERPRETING THE TEXT

The second necessary skill for practicing sound hermeneutics is ***interpretation***. Interpretation answers the question: **What does the passage mean?** Proper interpretation builds on good observation. Put another way, if one does not correctly observe, correct interpretation is impossible. If you were in a math class and carelessly looked at the white board at the front of the class and "observed", incorrectly, that it said <u>*7 - 3* =</u> you would conclude 4 was the correct answer, interpretation. If, however, the white board said, <u>*7 + 3* =</u> your answer would be completely different (at least let's hope so). And, correct interpretation will lead to accurate application. When you interpret, your goal is to discern the ***author's*** intended meaning, his one big idea in the text. When done, you will be able to express the meaning of the passage in your own words so that someone else can understand it. Before each step below, read the text.

I. Ask and Answer the Context Questions (cf. chapters 3-5)

    A. **Literary**: What type of literature is this?

    B. **Theological**: What is the ***dispensation*** (the two primary ones in the Bible, in terms of how much of scripture they cover are Law (Exodus 19 - Acts 1), and Church/Grace (Acts 2 - Revelation 19, with some exceptions)? What is the ***covenant*** (Mosaic or New) in effect? What ***people*** are addressed (Jews, Gentiles or Church. If Jews or Gentiles, are they saved or lost)?

133

C. **Historical**: What is the *author's* situation? The *recipients*? Is there anything to explore further?

D. **Book/Immediate**: What is the book *theme*? The author's/book's *purpose*? The theme of the paragraphs before and after the one I'm studying?

II. Write Your Initial Impression

A. What's your first impression about what the text means? What seems to be the one single idea of the text? Write that down as clearly as you can in one short sentence, two at the most.

B. Try to write your summary so that if someone else reads it, they would understand the meaning of the text.

III. Ask and Answer the Content Questions

Now, bombard the text with as many of the basic knowledge inductive questions as you can. These six basic inductive questions are the hinges on which the treasure chest lid of the Bible opens. Learn to seek their answers in every text you study.

A. *Who* wrote it? Who are the major people? Who are the people mentioned? To whom is the author speaking? About whom is the author speaking? The obvious "who's" are the proper names you will see. A good student will observe the less obvious who's. These will include terms like Pharisee, zealot, Sadducee, disciples, priests, etc. It will also include noticing pronouns, "I, me, they, we and you". Is the pronoun singular or plural?

B. *What* are the main events? What are the major ideas? What are the major teachings? What are the major people like? What does the author talk about the most? What are the major attitudes? What are the primary problems or challenges?

C. **When** did events occur? When will it happen? When did he say it? When did he do it? The more obvious when's will be "in the sixth year of …". The less obvious ones will be "on the third day", "the next day", "in the sixth hour". Even less obvious are words like, "afterward", "immediately" (a favorite of Mark's gospel) and "during" or "while". Notice all the time references you can in the text.

D. **Where** was this done? Where was this said? Where will it happen? Where did he go? Where did he come from? Again, the obvious where's are easy to find and most people see them. These include places like Antioch, Jerusalem, Mount Sinai. The less obvious, that often escape notice, are "on a roof", "under a tree", "in a tomb", "in a boat", and many more.

E. **Why** did this need to be written? Why was this mentioned? Why was so much or so little space devoted to this event or teaching? Why was this Scripture reference mentioned? Note: When asking the "why" question, the student will often get no answer from the text. If the text does not clearly state the why, do not add to God's word. Where it is silent you should be silent.

F. **How** was it done? How is this truth applied in the text? How did Jesus feed the 5000? At one level we can answer the question, He used the lunch of a boy to multiply food enough for everyone present. However, when pressed, we cannot say how Jesus did the multiplication other than to say, He is God and can do all things.

IV. Do Grammatical Studies as Needed (see chapters 8, 9)

A. Is there sentence structure that helps me understand the text?

B. What functional words, if any, are significant in this text? What do they reveal about the meaning?

C. What connecting words, if any, are significant in this text? What do they tell me?

D. What figures of speech do I need to clarify? What do they tell me about the meaning of the text?

E. What words require a word study? What does the word study tell me about the meaning of the text?

V. Compare Scripture with Scripture as Needed

A. Is there an Old Testament text to clarify with one from the New Testament?

B. Is there a New Testament text to clarify with one from the Old Testament?

C. Is there a need to compare or contrast your text with others?

VI. Clarify the Meaning

A. Develop a subject-complement statement.

Your analysis should lead to a clearer understanding of the passage as a whole. Initially, you read the passage and its context to understand the author's meaning. Then through analysis of the details, you tested your initial impression. Now you will make a statement of the **one** idea of the text in a subject and complement statement.

Subject is **what the text is talking about.**

Complement is **what the text says about the subject.**

1. Discern the subject

"Exactly what is the biblical writer talking about?" When you have a possible subject, go back through the passage and relate the subject to the details. Does the subject fit the parts? Is it too broad? Is it too narrow? Is your subject a clear and concise description of what the passage is talking about?

Your initial statement of a subject will often be too broad. To narrow it, try testing your subject with the inductive questions. A bit of verse tells us what those questions are:

> I had six faithful friends,
> They taught me all I knew,
> Their names are How and What and Why,
> When and Where and Who.

Applying these six questions to your proposed subject will help you be more exact. Take James 1:5-8 as an example:

"If any of you lacks wisdom, let him ask God, who gives to all men generously and without reproach, and it will be given to him. But let him ask in faith without any doubting, for the one who doubts is like the surf of the sea driven and tossed by the wind. For let not that man expect that he will receive anything from the Lord, being a double-minded man, unstable in all his ways."

An initial response to this paragraph might be that James is talking about ***wisdom***. While wisdom is a major element in the passage, it is too broad a subject. James does not discuss everything about wisdom and he discusses other key ideas.

Looking at the passage more closely, you find he is talking about "how to obtain wisdom", a more precise statement of the subject.

An awareness of the immediate context, however, enables you to limit the subject even further. The preceding paragraph, verses 2 – 4, teaches that "joy is the proper response to trials", and our paragraph extends that discussion. Therefore, a more complete subject for James 1:5-8 would be "how to obtain wisdom in the midst of trials".

All the details in the paragraph, directly or indirectly, relate to that subject. When a proposed subject accurately describes what the author is talking about, it illuminates the details of the passage; and the subject, in turn, will be illuminated by the details.

2. Determine the Complement

Having isolated the subject, you must now determine the complement, or what the text says about the subject. Complements complete the subject and make it into an idea. Often the complement becomes immediately obvious once you have stated the subject.

In James 1:5-8 the complement to the subject "how to obtain wisdom in the midst of trials" is "ask God for it in faith."

3. Write Out the Subject-Complement Sentence

A complete statement of the idea merely joins the subject with the complement: Wisdom in trials is obtained by asking God for it in faith. Everything else in the paragraph supports or elaborates that idea.

Check yourself with good commentaries such as the Bible Knowledge Commentary.

Keep or adjust your interpretation as needed. Write it out clearly.

Now You Try It # 13

Review this chapter including the following summary page. Read the next chapter of *Digging Deeper* and be prepared to discuss it. Write down any questions your reading generates. Read chapters 36-38 and 41-42 in *Living by the Book*. Finally, complete the assignment your teacher gives you and turn it in next class.

Homework Assignment #13:

Using your Final Project paragraph, write out a subject / complement statement for the paragraph in 20 words or less.

* Once again, two copies please.

Review / Summary of Chapter 13
INTERPRETING THE TEXT

Authorial intent – what was the author's original intent to communicate to his readers?

1. Ask and answer context questions. (Chapters 3 and 4)

2. Write your initial impression.

3. Ask and answer content questions.

4. Do grammatical studies as needed.

5. Compare scripture with scripture as needed

6. Clarify the meaning

    a. discern the subject
    b. determine the complement
    c. write out a subject / complement sentence

Chapter 14

Applying the Text

The next skill to develop is **_application_**. This answers the question: ***How does the meaning of the text work in life? What response does this passage suggest?*** Usually this is the first thing we want when we come to the Bible. However, it is the last step in the process. This is because proper application starts with our **_beliefs_**. Correct beliefs come from correct interpretations, which in turn will produce changed attitudes, values and behavior. Always remember that a legitimate application is a result of correct interpretation. When we misinterpret and so misapply, God gets upset! See his response to this in Job 42:7-9. Jesus was certainly talented in these skills. Look at an example from His life in Matthew 12:1-8.

The explanation below uses 2 Corinthians 9:7 as an example. It says, *"So let each one give as he purposes in his **_heart_**, not grudgingly or of necessity, for God loves a cheerful giver."*

I. Know the Text

    A. Write the meaning of the text in a subject/complement format. *God loves those who give purposefully and cheerfully.*

    B. Specify what primary areas of life the text addresses.

        1. Does it address attitudes? Values? Beliefs? Priorities? Motives? Relationships?

        2. Does it address behavior? Practices? Habits? Pleasures?

This text primarily addresses one's attitudes in giving.

C. State the abiding truths in the text.

1. Some passages transfer exactly – as does this one. Another example is "forgive one another" as in Eph. 4:32. The abiding truth is that "God commands Christians to forgive one another."

2. Some passages transfer only principles. A principle is a statement derived from Scripture that expresses unchanging truth relative to a particular subject. From Hebrews 11:7 you could say:

We aren't called to build an ark. However, we can state an unchanging truth (a principle) from the text. One principle is that "Faith in God accompanied by fear of God produces obedience to God."

D. Clarify the Purpose of the Text

What response did the author want from his readers who first read this text? Be specific.

The intended response was to motivate the Corinthians to give gladly and generously so that the collection for the poor churches in Judea would be bountiful and Paul's confidence in them rewarded.

II. Relate the Text to Your Situation

A. What circumstances or problem(s) does the text address? Write these out.

1. What exactly is the problem?
For an entire year the Corinthians, although they were in good financial shape, had failed to keep their promises to give to the poor Christians in Judea (2 Cr. 8:10, 14-15). This failure was caused by their low spiritual condition, lack of love and misunderstanding of grace (2 Cr. 8:7-9).

2. How did the problem arise?
They had committed to giving (8:10) but failed to follow through because of Paul's absence and the presence of false teachers (10:1-2, 11:7-10, 20, 12:14).

3. What type problem is it (theological, economic, relational, emotional, spiritual, etc.)? *Relational, emotional, spiritual*

4. What solution does the text offer by statement or implication? *Respond to God's spiritual grace by becoming financially gracious to others.*

B. What do you share with the original audience? Write out any parallels with the above.

Recipient of grace. Good economy. Rarely generous like God is. Missionaries and churches need my help.

C. What differs between your life and the original audience? Write them out.

No promise to give to saints in Jerusalem was made. I'm willing to give but sometimes afraid to give.

III. State Specific Responses to the Truth of the Text

A. If the text transfers straight way, let that be it (see 1A, 3B, 1C above).

God loves those who give purposefully and cheerfully, and we are to do so.

B. If there is a principle, state it clearly.

We reap spiritual benefits as we give with right motives.

C. Suggest SMART responses to the principle:

- **S**pecific responses: such as "*I will give*". Avoid at all cost generalities such as "*I need to start giving.*" If I were to step on my bathroom scale, which is electronic, and the number that flashed in the screen is not a number I like. I can say, "*I need to lose weight*"; that is only stating a need, but declaring any specific response such as "*I will lose weight*" is very different.
- **M**easurable: "*I will give $25 each week starting this Sunday*". I will lose 15 pounds. If it is not measureable, how will I know whether or not I have succeeded in meeting the goal? If I have not succeeded, did I get close (gave $25 ten out of fourteen weeks; I lost 11 pounds)?

- **A**ppropriate to your situation: *$25 is 15% of my weekly income – that's an appropriate starting place.* That is not appropriate for some people. Those who make millions of dollars should consider giving a greater percentage. A thin person can't lose 50 pounds.
- **R**elational: it builds your love for God and / or people and your dependence on God. *"I will trust God to provide my needs and I will thank Him each time I write the check."*
- **T**ransfer life habits: Always focus on what you will start, not what you want to stop. Don't say, *"I want to stop spending too much on pizza, so I can give."* Say, *"I will give you $25 each week starting this Sunday."*

Let's try two in class using Ephesians 4:29 as our scripture.

Ephesians 4:29

"Let no unwholesome word proceed from your mouth, but only such a word as is good for edification according to the need of the moment, so that it will give grace to those who hear."

Is it Specific? (Avoid general statements or observations)

Is it Measurable? (How so? If not, what would make it measurable?)

Is it Appropriate? (Appropriate of me? Others? If not, how could it be?)

Review/Summary of Chapter 14

1. Know the text:
    A. Before ever progressing to application complete a subject/ compliment statement of the passage.
    B. What response did the author want his original readers to offer?
    C. Clarify the purpose of the text. What response did the author expect/desire from his readers?

2. Relate the text to your situation:
    A. What circumstances or problems does the text address?
    B. What do you share with original audience?
    C. What differs between you and original audience?
3. State specific responses to the truth of the text: **S.M.A.R.T.**
    A. Specific – What will be done?
    B. Measurable – How can I/we/they measure it?
    C. Appropriate – Is that appropriate for me/them?
    D. Relational – Does is focus on relationships with God and/or others?
    E. Transfer life habits – What will I/we/they start doing?

> **NOW YOU TRY #14**
> Read chapters 39, 40, and 43-45 in *Living by the Book.* Additionally…
>
> Using the passage of Scripture you have chosen from the book of Philippians for your final project create at least two (2) S.M.A.R.T. applications. With each one, be sure that it accurately reflects the subject/compliment statement you have developed. Make one of the applications personal (e.g., "I will…"). The second application may be personal or more corporate (group) centered (e.g., "I challenge you all to…").

1. Application #1…

2. Application #2…

Chapter 15
THE REARVIEW MIRROR: Summarizing the process of Digging Deeper

Congratulations for hanging in there for the past fourteen chapters! This final chapter is an overview, a summary of the ground we've covered recently. Hopefully the review will help crystalize some truth clearly in your mind and then your practice of studying the Bible.

1. DO YOU READ WELL?

- Unsaved people cannot be good students of the Word of God. Regeneration is the foundation upon which good hermeneutics rests (John 3:1-16; 1 Cor. 2:14, 15). Being saved does not ensure good hermeneutics, it just ensures that it is possible.

- To effectively build upon the foundation of new life in Christ, the believer will need to possess 3 vital attitudes: A <u>desire</u> for God's truth, a <u>dependence</u> upon the Holy Spirit, and a <u>diligence</u> to study the Word.

- There are some wonderful benefits to Bible study. Among them are: Steady growth, spiritual maturity, spiritual effectiveness, and protection from error and danger.

- Inductive Bible study occurs as the reader <u>observes</u> a particular <u>text</u> of Scripture in order to come to a <u>conclusion</u> (interpretation).

2. THE PRINCIPLE OF PLAIN MEANING

- We should take words at face value (literally). Normally a text of Scripture has only one meaning. Our goal should be to discover God's message (authorial intent) NOT what the passage means to me.

- There are some common mistakes people make when reading the Bible. Among them are: Spiritualizing the text; importing ideas into the text; concluding the interpretation without actually reading the passage.

- To guard against error, the interpreter can check her conclusions: The most obvious meaning is usually the correct one; The correct meaning will be consistent with the immediate context and the rest of the Bible; when a passage appears to have more than one interpretation, choose the simplest; finally, check your finished work with a good commentary.

3, 4 & 5 PRINCIPLE OF CONTEXT

- Context is the environment in which the passage of Scripture rests. It could well be described as the setting. Every passage of the Bible has several contexts: Literary context is the type of literature you are reading. Theological context addresses the dispensation (era, administration, timeframe) your passage occurred in; the covenant deals with the specific regulations/agreement in place between God and man in that time/era; people group answers the question of what group of people was the passage written to? Jews, Gentiles or the church?

- Historical context addresses two principles, the author's situation at the time of writing and the original reader's situation at the time of writing.

- The final context is the book context. Here the theme (what the book is about) and purpose (why the book was written) are discovered. Usually they are discovered by multiple readings of the entire book.

- Immediate context deals with the paragraph before and after the one you are studying. How do these two paragraphs influence the meaning of your passage?

6 & 7 THE PRINCIPLE OF GRAMMAR

- Meaning is expressed through the relationships of words in a sentence. Be careful to observe functional words in a sentence (subject, verb, and object).

- Sentence and paragraph structure are often seen through repetition, contrast, comparison, continuation, and summarization.

- Prepositions tell you where the action or relationships take place. Conjunctions connect one thought with another.

- Nouns are persons, places, things or qualities. They can be common nouns or proper nouns (capitalized – as in names and places).

- A gerund is a "verbal noun" that usually includes some form of action.

- Pronouns are words that take the place of nouns. They might be personal, indefinite, reflexive, interrogative or possessive.

- Verbs are words that describe action or state of being.

- Adjectives are words that modify or describe nouns or other adjectives. They limit the use of nouns or pronouns.

- Adverbs often in in "ly" (e.g., "quickly" or "suddenly", etc.) and describe verbs, other adverbs or adjectives.

8 & 9. WORD MEANING

- Word Studies enable the student of Scripture to access the original Greek or Hebrew to discover possible meanings of specific words in a passage of the Bible.

- The word chosen by the student for a Word Study should be a word that is central to understanding the meaning of the passage and/or a word whose meaning is unknown to the student.

- The Word Study process (see appendix) should be followed in its entirety.

- Range of meaning refers to semantic range. What are all the possible ways the word you are studying was used in the New Testament (or Old Testament, if conducting a Hebrew Word Study)?

- Consulting helpful resources such as Vine's Expository Dictionary of New Testament Words (Greek) or Theological Wordbook of the Old Testament (T.W.O.T.) for Hebrew words will be beneficial.

10. LITERALLY? UNSTANDING FIGURATIVE LANGUAGE

- Figures of speech use non-literal imagery to convey literal truths, thus they do not violate the principle of plain meaning (literal interpretation).

- When considering a figure of speech, determine the <u>image</u> (non-literal "picture" – e.g., "flying Porsche"), the <u>referent</u> (who or what does the image refer to?) and finally, the <u>interpretation</u>. What did the author intend to convey when he wrote this figure of speech?

11. THE PRINCIPLE OF RELATED SCRIPTURE

- The Bible is the best commentary on the Bible. When considering the interpretation of any one passage of Scripture, it is wise to consider what the rest of the Bible says about that idea/doctrine. Put another way, no one passage of Scripture contains all the truth about that concept.

- Consider what the other parts/sections of the Bible have to say about your text/topic (Old Testament compared to New Testament and vice versa).

- How do contrasting truths help modify and/or inform your interpretation of the passage (e.g. Jesus was fully human after His incarnation, yet He has always been divine and is eternal)?

12. OBSERVING THE TEXT

- To read better, do the following: Read in a quiet, well lit place with a translation of the Bible that you generally understand. Read with feeling, at conversational speed, to get the main point, to get the big picture, and repeatedly.

- You will get more out of your Bible reading as you observe the following: Things that are emphasized, repeated, alike, different/unlike, and true-to-life.

13. INTERPRETING THE TEXT

- Ask and answer the **context** questions (chapters 3 & 4) – Literary, theological, historical, and book contexts.

- Ask and answer **content** questions (who, what, when, where, why, and how?). Use diligence to see beyond the obvious and peel back the easily seen layers to get to the core of the content of the passage.

- Do grammatical studies (Word Studies) as needed.

- Compare Scripture with Scripture. What other places in the Bible address this same concept? What contrasting ideas might help inform your interpretation?

- Clarify your paragraph by creating a subject/compliment statement. It should be concise (15 words or less). In your subject/compliment statement you should capture what the passage is all about and what the passage says about that main idea.

14. APPLYING THE TEXT

- Know the text, if you've not developed a subject/compliment statement, do so ***before*** attempting any applications.

- Create specific responses to the truth of the text that are S.M.A.R.T. (specific, measurable, appropriate, relational, and that transfer life habits).

NEXT STEPS...

Learning to study the Bible well is in many ways like training to be an Olympic athlete. Wanting to be a champion won't make you one – Olympic medalists train, discipline themselves and consistently employ good coaches and technique.

That's how it is with good Bible study. The diligent, consistent use of the techniques you learned this quarter will make you skillful in "handling accurately the word of truth." You probably agree that this class hasn't been easy. It wasn't, but you have finished! Congratulations! Nothing worth doing well is easy – especially in the spiritual life. The world, the flesh, the devil and carnal brothers always resist us.

So where do you go from here? Here are some suggestions.

- Take the next class in the curriculum, Hermeneutics 1. It will reinforce concepts learned in this course and teach further principles to help you to interpret the Bible with greater accuracy and confidence.
Review these notes and select other texts to practice on other than those in the "You Try It" sections. You've studied the book of Philippians in this course. There are 65 other books in the English Bible. Choose another one and begin studying it. Don't get discouraged at the thought that you have 65 more books to study. If you study a book of the Bible for three months and then move on to another, in two years you will have studied eight books in detail, that's eight more than you would have mastered had you not studied at all.

- To begin with it would be wise to choose shorter books, such as Ephesians, Colossians or James, than a much longer book, such as Isaiah or Ezekiel until you become more confident and skilled.

- Study this workbook with a group. If you teach it, you will learn even more. At the same time, the interaction will teach you too. Why not go to your pastor, or the appropriate person, and ask if you might teach the material you have learned in this course? When you are the teacher, it will force you to study and grow.

- Above all, don't think you are done with the course because you finished and passed it. The real tests are just beginning. Remember and respond to Jesus' words in Matthew 7:24:

> *"Therefore, whoever **hears these sayings of mine and does them**,*
> I will liken him to a wise man who built his house on the rock..."

APPENDICES

1. Word Study process
2. Final project check list
3. Recommended commentary list

WORD STUDY PROCESS

WORD STUDY CHECK LIST

1. **Choose a word**…what is the word you will study? Include the originating reference.

2. **Look up the word in your concordance** (make sure you are using the same translation of a concordance as you are the Bible – NAS to NAS or KJV to KJV – compare "apples to apples")

3. What is the NUMBER associated with the word? Write down the **NUMBER**.

4. In the back of the concordance, **look up the number in the correct dictionary** (Hebrew for Old Testament words; Greek for New Testament words) AND write down the definition of the word being studied.

5. Using your concordance, is your **word (same number) used elsewhere in the same book** of the Bible (Philippians)?

6. Is your **word used elsewhere** (another book of the Bible) **by the same author** (Paul)? If yes, where and how often? Look these up and read carefully. Jot down the answer.

7. Look up your word in **Vine's Expository Dictionary** (New Testament words) OR **Wilson's Word Studies** (Old Testament words). What does this resource say?

8. What is the **range of meaning** for the word? FOR EXAMPLE, the word "save" can mean, go to heaven, to preserve from physical harm, to rescue from illness, to make well or whole. Jot down all the possibilities for your word.

9. Given the context, what is **your interpretation of the word in this context**?

10. What does a good commentary say about this word and your interpretation?

FINAL PROJECT CHECKLIST

This class is a methods course. You learn best by practicing the principles taught in this course and built upon each week through your homework. Most of the assignments you have already done, though you may want to improve upon them before submitting it as a part of your final project.

1. In detail, fill out the first three context boxes (literary, theological, and historical) for the book of Philippians. [It need ***not*** be in chart form].

2. Book context, the last of the four contexts includes ***theme***, ***purpose*** and a ***book outline*** for Philippians.

3. Turn in one figure of speech from the book of Philippians, stating what the **image** and **referent** are as well as an **interpretation** in its context.

4. **Choose any one paragraph** in the book of Philippians to be your teaching/preaching passage for the remainder of the final project.

5. Develop an **outline** of the passage chosen (#4 above) as though you were going to teach/preach it (main points and sub points, if appropriate).

6. Do at least one **word study** from the passage (#4 above). Your word study must include all the steps outlined in a proper word study (see Word Study process appendix).

7. Create at least **two (2) SMART applications** for your life and the lives of those you might teach using the passage you have chosen (#4 above).

RECOMMENDED COMMENTARY LIST

A commentary is merely another person's comments, his/her interpretation of a passage. They are not inspired, though some are clearly better than others. There are literally thousands of commentaries that could be purchased, but many are useless. The following are a few that cover many books of the Bible, rather than commentaries on each book of the Bible (for example, a New Testament commentary versus a commentary on the book of Romans).

1. *Bible Knowledge Commentary*, Edited by John Walvoord and Roy B. Zuck. Two volume set on the entire Bible. Authored by Dallas Theological Seminary professors. Published by Victor books, 1983.

2. *Believer's Bible Commentary,* William McDonald and Arthur Farstad. One volume on the entire Bible. Published by Thomas Nelson, 1995.

3. *The Bible Exposition Commentary,* by Warren W. Wiersbe. This is a six-volume commentary of the entire Bible. Published by Victor books 1998. There are two volumes on the New Testament and four on the Old Testament.

If you are interested in single volume commentaries, I highly recommend the Charles R. Swindoll series on the New Testament, *New Testament Insights*. It is very well done and combines both scholarship and practical insight and application. They are published by Zondervan.

About the author...

Bill Korver served in local church ministry for 22 years, as an assistant pastor and a church planter/senior pastor. He served as an adjunct professor at Carolina College of Biblical Studies (CCBS) from 1990 until 2003. Since 2004 he has served as the president of CCBS. He holds degrees from Southeastern Bible College (B.A. & M.A.), Luther Rice University (M.Div.) and Liberty University (D.Min.). It has been his privilege to teach the contents of this workbook more than 60 times to several hundred CCBS students and others in various settings. He is married to Marcia and has three grown children and several grandchildren. He enjoys outdoor projects, hunting as well as reading theology, biographies and mysteries.

www.ingramcontent.com/pod-product-compliance
Lightning Source LLC
Chambersburg PA
CBHW060528010526
44110CB00052B/2531